PRO
CHOICES

WHAT TO DO WHEN YOU DON'T KNOW WHAT TO DO

D1091942

Anne Gimenez

Tulsa, OK

20 19 18 17   10 9 8 7 6 5 4 3 2 1

ProChoices:
What to Do When You Don't Know What to Do
Copyright © 2017 by Anne Gimenez

ISBN: 978-1-68031-166-2

Published by Harrison House Publishers
Tulsa, Oklahoma 74145
www.harrisonhouse.com

Dedication

This book is dedicated to those seekers out there trying to find understanding and truth for their lives today.

I also want to dedicate this book to "my girls":
Robin Anne, Amelia Anne-Elizabeth and Asia Lily-Anne.

You are the lights of my life. What a joy you are to me!
As you walk through this journey called life,
remember to always make the *right choice!*

Contents

Introduction

I don't know if you know how to live a righteous life, but I really didn't. I didn't know exactly what a righteous life would look like in my daily reality. One night in bed, I began to think about Matthew 6:25: "Take no thought for your life, what ye shall eat, or what ye shall drink; nor yet for your body, what ye shall put on. Is not the life more than meat, and the body than raiment?" This verse tells me that the eternal life on the inside of me is more important than any concern in my natural life.

My mind then skipped down to Matthew 6:33: "But seek ye first the kingdom of God, and his righteousness; and all these things shall be added unto you." This was a familiar verse. I preached the kingdom and sought the King. I got up every morning, walked around my living room, raised my hands, and shouted at the top of my voice, "Hallelujah! The kingdom of God is here, and I'm in it!"

But that night, I saw Matthew 6:33 in a different way. I had been taught and now taught others to seek first (meaning first in time, place, or rank) the kingdom of God, but I'd never thought about seeking *His righteousness*. The verse says to seek God's kingdom AND His righteousness. THEN "all these things shall be added unto you." Nobody ever told me to seek His righteousness, not that I would have known how to do that, anyway!

I began to ponder the word *righteous*, wondering exactly what it means. When I looked up the word in the dictionary, the definition talked about virtue, morality, justice, honesty, and decency. Those were all good words, but there was something more working in my spirit, something that wasn't satisfied. Then I read this portion of the definition: *correctness of thinking, feeling, and acting.*

Righteousness *is* correctness of thinking, feeling, and acting. To be righteous, everything you think, feel, and do (including what you say) should be right with God. Now I know that society pressures us to be "politically correct," but political ideas can change from day to day or even hour to hour. That's why Christians live by the Word of God and the Holy Spirit. God's Word stands forever, and His Spirit knows all things. We can be secure and at peace when we follow God's Word and the leading of the Holy Spirit.

After I saw that the definition of righteousness includes correct thinking, feeling, and acting, the word *righteous* kept resonating in my spirit: *righteous, righteous, righteous.* Finally, the light bulb went on in my brain. I heard *righteous* as "right choices." The Holy Spirit was teaching me that seeking God's righteousness means simply making right choices!

Jesus always made the right decision because He did only what He saw His Father doing (John 5:19). Ephesians 5:1 commands us to imitate our Father God. All His choices are right. We are to choose what He would choose, to agree with Him and do His will. That doesn't just mean at church, either! God is with us all the time, everywhere. In everything we think, say, feel, and do, we are to be like our Father God and make right choices.

Once I had this revelation of right choices, I took action to really cement it into my life. I made a list of everything I had done recently. Had I made the right decisions? I knew that when I made the right choice, I was seeking God's righteousness. I was imitating Him and becoming more like Jesus. I thought, *I need to make the right choice, which might not be the convenient choice or the easy choice. The right choice sometimes hurts. The right choice can make me flinch. The right choice can cost me something I hold dear.*

I looked at the times I'd been "too tired" to make the right choice. I felt guilty afterward and even more tired. I understood that my guilt came from disobedience, but why was my exhaustion even greater? When I was not seeking *His* righteousness, I also was not seeking *His* strength to do *His* will. So, of course, I felt even more tired! In addition, nothing weighs you down more than regret over making the wrong decision.

I thought about the times people told me they knew what God wanted them to do, but then I watched them do just the opposite. I never looked at those instances as unrighteous acts; I just saw them as disobedience or an error in judgment. Now I realized that making the wrong choice was not seeking the kingdom of God and His righteousness. The righteous are supposed to make right choices. This is what God wants—but it isn't always what we want.

Making right choices can seem very hard when you're making them, but life is so much easier after you do what is right. Life just gets harder and more complicated when you make a wrong decision. In the end, the right choice becomes the easiest because you are right with God, with yourself, and with others. This enables God to move freely on your behalf.

Think of your own life. When God shows you that someone has a need, and the Holy Spirit moves you to do something about it, do you? When you meet someone new at work, do you make the effort to get to know them, or do you make excuses like, "I'm too busy"?

Sometimes we just don't like someone and use that as an excuse not to talk to them or pray for them. "I can't stand her personality. I know his family, and all those people are up to no good." If this is the case, you need to talk with God about that person! He's the only One who really knows what's going on. Your prayers and friendship may be the key to someone's salvation and freedom.

When I connected my choices to seeking first God's righteousness, even the little choices took on a whole new significance. Now, I see everything I choose to think, everything I say, feel, and do as so important. More and more, I see the lasting impact of every decision I make. My choices determine how I mature in the Lord, whether or not I accomplish His will for my life, and how I affect the lives of others. Most importantly, right choices bring the power of God into my life!

I encourage you to check your choices every day. Did you seek God's righteousness by making right choices? How did things turn out? Make it a habit to check your choices at a set time every day, and over time, you will be more conscious of whether your choices match up with what God wants as you go about your daily life.

As you read on, I pray you will get a deeper understanding of how and why Jesus told us to seek first both the kingdom of God and His righteousness. I know this understanding will transform your life as it has mine!

1

....

The Power
of Right Choices

It sounds so simple. We are to do the right thing, not the
wrong thing. Yet if it's so simple, why do we keep doing the
wrong thing? Why do some Christians continue to make a mess
of their lives? I don't think any of us grow up praying for that!

I decided to look closely at the process of making a choice.
Was there some way I could ensure that I would make the right
decision in every situation?

The Holy Spirit had me begin with Proverbs 23:7, which
says that what we *think* is what we *become*.

The Almighty Thought

Everything that comes out of our mouths and every action
we take begins with a thought. As righteous folks, we should
make right choices; but to do that, we must think righteous

thoughts. We need to think like our Father, the Almighty God. Our thoughts ought to be Almighty thoughts! There's a double meaning in that statement. Our thoughts should reflect those of the Almighty, but also, because our thoughts direct our decisions, our thoughts are "almighty" in our lives. Stop right now and ask yourself, "Is what I'm dwelling on and meditating about reflecting what God loves and wants to accomplish?"

Our thoughts are almighty because they determine everything we say and do. Every choice comes from a thought, so we need to choose the right thoughts—Almighty God's thoughts—if we want to seek God's righteousness in every area of our lives.

The devil and the world tell you that every thought you have is yours, but the Bible tells you the truth: God and the enemy both speak to you. You choose whose thoughts you're going to go with, and these thoughts then become your thoughts. Worshipping and serving God begins in your thought life.

We all choose our thoughts. If we're stuck on something sinful, deceptive, or distracting, it's because we've chosen to stay stuck in a demonic rut. Let's take the example of just not liking someone. We *choose* to think of that person in negative ways: *I just don't like her. I mean, the way she talks. Just her tone of voice grates on my nerves. And the way she behaves! It's like she was born in a barn or something.* On and on we go, remembering every horrible thing that person ever said or did. We choose to go down that path, and it isn't a path of righteousness! Seeking God's righteousness means we ask God, "What are You thinking about this person?" When I have a negative reaction to someone, I have a choice. I can go with it or I can ask the Lord to show me why I react to the person the way I do. Maybe I'm the one with the problem and not him or her! Maybe the Holy Spirit brought that person into my life to expose some fault or weakness in me. Sometimes when I've prayed through these situations, the person I initially disliked became one of my best friends! Think what I would have missed if I hadn't gone to the Lord, if I hadn't made the right choice.

I choose my thoughts. I had known this truth for years, but now it took on a whole new meaning to me. If I am thinking about something that has never happened and possibly never will happen, and the image of that situation is making me anxious and fearful, I need to seek God's righteousness and stop those thoughts. How many times does the Word say, "Fear not, for God is with you"? We are not supposed to walk around obsessed with everything that could go wrong in our lives, in the world, or in our families. God is always with us, His Word and His promises are for us, and we have no reason to fear.

Even when I'm in a situation where my flesh is shaking with fear on the outside of me, I can seek His righteousness on the inside of me. I can choose to think on all His blessings and His mighty power that are working for me. Choosing the Almighty's thoughts in the midst of a storm keeps my inner being at peace, even when my flesh is weak and going crazy. This is one of the miracles of being a child of God!

There are times when my mind begins to wander, especially when I'm tired. Isn't that a great expression? In these times, my mind wanders away from what it should be thinking. Seeking God's righteousness at that moment means cutting off wandering thoughts and choosing to think the way the Bible tells me to think:

Whatsoever things are true, whatsoever things are honest, whatsoever things are just, whatsoever things are pure, whatsoever things are lovely, whatsoever things are of good report;

if there be any virtue, and if there be any praise, think on these things.

Philippians 4:8

When I choose to think about things that are true, honest, just, pure, lovely, of good report (not gossip or rumor)—things that are virtuous and praiseworthy—my whole perspective changes. Why? Because I'm choosing to think like my Father God and come into full agreement with Him. Now my problems don't seem so big because He is the Almighty!

To make right choices, first you have to straighten out your thinking. Everything you say and do begins with a thought or comes from a thought pattern. You don't just walk up and insult your boss to his face one day. You thought about it. You entertained images of giving him a piece of your mind. After thinking those devilish thoughts long enough, you could be sure the devil would give you an opportunity to say exactly what you'd been thinking!

A good man out of the good treasure of his heart bringeth forth that which is good; and an evil man out of the evil treasure of his heart bringeth forth that which is evil: for of the abundance of the heart his mouth speaketh.

Luke 6:45

You have a good heart because God made you righteous through the precious blood of Jesus Christ. Now you need to think out of your good heart. That takes the discipline of making right choices. Reject thoughts that aren't acceptable to God and choose thoughts in line with His Word and Spirit. Almighty thoughts keep your attitude right, and then your words will be right too.

Speak No Evil

Your words are powerful. They can build someone up or bring someone down. They can bring someone to their senses or tear them to pieces. Your words can lovingly correct, instruct, and set a person on a better path in life. The words you speak in prayer, when they are inspired by God's Word and will, can change the world around you. Jesus said that if you believe what you say, you will have it.

> For verily I say unto you, That whosoever shall say unto this mountain, Be thou removed, and be thou cast into the sea; and shall not doubt in his heart, but shall believe that those things which he saith shall come to pass; he shall have whatsoever he saith.
>
> Therefore I say unto you, What things soever ye desire, when ye pray, believe that ye receive them, and ye shall have them.
>
> Mark 11:23-24

This truth from God's Word should be a reminder that your words are so powerful, you should think twice before you open your mouth to speak. You never know the lasting impact your words will have. I'm not just talking about moving mountains; your words affect the course of your own life, too.

> For he that will love life, and see good days, let him refrain his tongue from evil, and his lips that they speak no guile.
>
> 1 Peter 3:10

Do you love life? Do you want to live a good life, even a great one? This verse holds the key to doing just that. This is not talking about the world's idea of life, merely breathing and walking around doing things. This verse is talking about eternal life, the life of God inside you. If you love life—everlasting life—and you want to see good days full of unspeakable joy and glory, there is something you need to do: Refrain your tongue from evil and speak no guile.

Speak what the Holy Spirit prompts you to speak, talking from your spirit and not from your old, sinful nature. Then you won't say evil, wicked things. Wickedness includes everything that is base and sinful, troublesome, destructive, depraved, and immoral.

We are also to speak no guile. To speak guile is to be cunning and sly, underhanded and manipulative. It is speaking in such a way as to get people to do what we want them to do. It's being dishonest and crafty. As children of God, we need to be up-front and open with people. God always speaks honestly, and we should too.

Let him eschew evil, and do good; let him seek peace, and ensue it.

1 Peter 3:11

We are to "eschew" evil, which means to "shoo" it away! We cannot linger on any thought that is against God's Word or gives us a check in our spirits. When we are tempted to say something that's wrong, we need to choose to keep our mouths shut or say the right thing instead.

When someone offends you, hurts you, or makes you angry, you have a choice. You can immediately respond with a cutting remark, or you can smile and turn away without responding. Did you know that? You don't have to defend yourself. All you have to do is follow the Holy Spirit. He will either have you forgive as you go on or forgive as you say something nice to the one who wronged you. You may feel like slapping that person, but you can "eschew" that impulse and walk away in peace. I didn't say this was easy, but with God, ALL things are possible!

Most of us stumble when we think what we are doing is unimportant. For example, when I'm standing in line for long periods of time to accomplish a mundane task, I think, *I could be doing some really important things right now. This is a waste of time. These people are so slow.* I may then turn to the other people in the line and make a joke that is really nothing more than a complaint about my situation. By the time it's my turn to be served, I'm not my usual nice self to the person who waits on me. I may speak the right words, but my attitude toward them is wrong.

When I reflected on this situation, I realized I was not seeking first God's righteousness, and I missed an opportunity to touch people with His love and kindness. Who knows what some of those people in the line and the person helping me might have been going through? My words might have made a difference.

For the eyes of the Lord are over the righteous, and his ears are open unto their prayers: but the face of the Lord is against them that do evil.

1 Peter 3:12

Who is God looking at? Who is He paying attention to? You! You are the righteous. If His eyes are over you, then His face is turned toward you. He's very interested in everything you say. That's why you need to pay attention to what is coming out of your mouth. Is it evil or good? Guile or honesty? Does God see you turn away from evil and guile, or does He see you give in to your flesh and let someone have it? God is watching.

God's not sitting up there waiting to swat you every time you make a mistake. His eyes are watching over you like a protective, caring Father. He wants to help you make the right decision in every situation. First Peter 3:12 says His ears are open to your prayers. The first right choice you can ever make is turning away from evil and turning to God, praying for His help and His wisdom. That is the best right choice you can make!

The worst choice you can make is to turn away from God. Our righteous Father cannot hear prayers that come from a heart that has turned away from Him and has decided to speak evil things. You may say of your words, "But it was the truth!" But was it what the Holy Spirit wanted you to say? Was it said after much prayer and in His love?

God won't answer the prayers of those who use the truth in a dishonest or self-serving way. Speaking the truth with a bad attitude is evil. Remember, the devil uses the truth to accuse us and condemn us. He wants to destroy us with it, and he delights in getting Christians to attack people (and each other) with the truth. Jesus speaks the truth in love to set us free, and He's the model we should follow.

If you wonder why your prayers aren't getting answered or why your life is filled with strife and misery, you need to determine if you are making right choices in what you say. Ask the Holy Spirit to show you where you've missed it, and then begin making the right choices as you speak. That mountain of strife and misery has got to move!

Do the Right Thing

Once you are aware that you are thinking right and speaking right, you need to make sure your actions reflect your right thoughts and words. Recently, I was challenged in this area. I like to look at Facebook on my phone. I also check my email and text messages on my phone, so I spend a lot of time looking at my phone. One day I was having a really good time, when I heard the gentle voice of the Holy Spirit say, "That's enough."

I immediately knew I had to make a choice. I liked what I was doing. I liked what I was seeing. I liked checking out all my friends' posts about what was going on in their lives. But in my spirit, I felt the Lord saying, "You have something else to do."

I said, "Oh, all right." I didn't make a face, but I had to force myself to make the right choice. God was telling me to get back to studying for the message I was going to give that week. I love to study God's Word, but at that moment, I preferred to study Facebook! In obedience, I put my phone away. So much of what you are reading in this book came from that simple act of doing the right thing. Thank God I did!

And who is he that will harm you, if ye be followers of that which is good?

1 Peter 3:13

Loving and serving the Lord means doing what He asks you to do, and your obedience keeps you safe. The moment I chose to study God's Word instead of being on Facebook, I made it impossible for the enemy to harm me. I shudder to think what might have happened if I had ignored the voice of the Holy Spirit and followed my own desires instead of seeking God's righteousness. You can only feel truly safe and secure when you make the right choice by obeying His voice.

It's simple: We are to do the right thing as followers of Christ. Do you remember when we all wore wristbands that said "WWJD" (What Would Jesus Do)? If you're in a quandary about what to do, just think *WWJD*. Since you are in Him and He is in you, He is right there to help you make the right choice.

When I was a teenager, I made a right choice that cost me a lot for a season, but it gave me a much better life in the long run. I was engaged to my high school sweetheart, who went to serve in the Korean War. By the time he returned, I had been born again and filled with the Holy Spirit. He wasn't, and so I told him all about Jesus and how I wanted to live my life for Him. I said, "I love you enough to tell you the truth. You need Jesus. If you'll serve God with me, then let's get married. I want to raise my children to love God. If you don't, I can't marry you."

I was young in the Lord, but I had read the verse of scripture that said, "Be ye not unequally yoked together with unbelievers: for what fellowship hath righteousness with unrighteousness? and what communion hath light with darkness?" (2 Corinthians 6:14). This young man didn't want Jesus in his life, and so my heart was broken over choosing not to marry him. But I was safe. I was secure.

For ten years it was hard as my friends were getting married and having babies, but I trusted God and focused on doing whatever He wanted me to do. As I was serving the Lord, I met and married John Gimenez. We had a wonderful life with Jesus. John has gone on to Heaven now, but what we had is still going on today through our daughter and her family, the ministry we built together, and all our spiritual sons and daughters. Praise God! I'm so glad I made the right choice. Choosing to wait for God's best has brought tremendous happiness to me.

The kind of lasting satisfaction and joy I'm talking about comes from right thinking, speaking, and acting. It comes because you seek first God's righteousness, and then He blesses you by adding everything you need to succeed in life. As I said before, it isn't always easy, but God will give you the grace to make the right choices.

2

God's Grace and Goodness

The Church has recently rediscovered the power of God's grace. That's a good thing, so long as we understand that God's grace is not provided to allow us to get away with making wrong choices. God's grace gives us the ability to make the right choices, to live a righteous life that reveals God's goodness to everyone around us.

Our witness for Jesus goes right out the window if our friends, family, neighbors, and co-workers see us making wrong choices. I'm not talking about making innocent mistakes or doing something we didn't know was wrong. I'm talking about doing something we know is wrong. I don't see any reference in the Bible to "greasy grace." Nowhere does it say to sin now and pray later. Again and again it says, "Sin not," or "Go and sin no more," or "Abide in God's Word. Live by the Spirit and not the flesh."

God's amazing grace is available to us in every decision. When I sit down to a meal in a restaurant, I have to decide whether I will eat the pie or the sugar-free JELL-O. Will I stay on my diet, or will I cheat a little? I know what the right choice is! I am happy, healthy, and set a good example for others when I draw upon God's grace to do the right thing and take care of my body. Now you may say, "Well that's just a little thing," but people notice the little things as much as the big things. If they see you doing right in the little stuff, they will trust you with the big stuff—just like God does (Matthew 25:21).

I am amazed at what I hear believers say and watch them do. "Well, I'm just looking. I'm not touching. It's no sin to think about that man's wife." That's not true, and it's certainly not living in God's grace. That's rejecting God's grace! His grace empowers you to turn away from the temptation that Jesus said begins in the heart with a thought or image you choose to dwell on. Noticing a handsome man or beautiful woman who is not your spouse is not a sin, but continuing to think about that person is!

The choices we make reflect our relationship with God. They reveal to everyone around us whether or not we are serving Him. No one will see the grace of God if they don't see it working in us. For example, when we pay off a debt instead of buying something we really don't need, we demonstrate God's empowering grace. But if we spend our money on ourselves or on others to impress them, going deeper into debt, we are saying, "The grace of God has no power in my life."

If sports, the arts, or other activities are more important than raising our children in church and instructing them in the things of God, then we are encouraging our kids to turn from the Lord and get into all kinds of trouble. This does not just bring trouble to us, but also to the schools they attend, to their friends and their friends' families, and to the jobs they do out in the world. On the other hand, if we make the right choice to instruct our children in the things of God, people will see the grace of God in our families through the good behavior of our children. We can be secure and confident when they leave home, knowing God is with them as they love and serve Him in His grace.

When I had been in ministry just a very short time, God told me to go back home to Corpus Christi, Texas. He said He wanted to teach me something there, and He would tell me when I could leave. I figured I was very teachable and, therefore, shouldn't be there more than a few weeks. *Eight and a half years later*, the Lord finally moved on my heart and told me I could leave!

At the beginning of that eight years, I said to my best friend, "I know it is the will of God for me to be here, but I can hardly stand it." As I drove away from her house, the Holy Spirit began to impart God's grace to me through His Word. He said, "Bitter and sweet water cannot come out of the same fountain." He was quoting James 3:11, and that word went right through me.

I realized that one side of my mouth was saying, "I know this is God's will for my life," while the other side of my mouth was saying, "I can hardly stand it." God's will may not be easy, but it is always right and good. So I repented and said, "Lord, what do You want me to say?"

He said, "I want you to say what David said."

I asked, "What did David say?"

"I delight to do thy will, oh my God" (Psalm 40:8).

Saying that took me three days! The first day the statement sounded something like, "I. Delight. To do. Thy will, oh God."

The second day it was more like, "I delight to do thy will, oh God?" By the third day, I finally was able to say, "I delight to do Your will, God. I surrender." That's when I began to learn what the Lord wanted to teach me. Looking back, I recognize that when I chose to repent and surrender my will to God's, I was seeking His righteousness and receiving His grace. Now I know how to make right choices!

In God's grace, you can make the right choice and then act on it. If you're pondering a decision, pray and ask Him for direction. When He shows you the right thing to do, don't pay attention to your emotions or what your flesh wants. Draw on His miracle-working grace and do what's right. Then you can have faith in God for your future.

In one of my Bibles, I wrote on the opening page, "Always do the right thing." This was a great place for that reminder because if you don't know what the right thing might be, you can always go to the Word of God to check it out. If you need more help, ask your pastor or a mature brother or sister in the Lord to pray with you. Always try to make the right decision in what you think, say, and do. Then God's eyes will be over you, ready and willing to answer your prayers.

People Are Looking for God's Goodness

When people know you are a Christian, their eyes will be on you to see what you will think, speak and do. They're looking to see if you are the real deal or a hypocrite. Will you just talk the talk, or will you walk the walk? Many unbelievers are hoping to see you make wrong choices, because then they feel superior to you, and they aren't challenged to confront their sin and need for a Savior. But there are a lot of folks out there who are literally dying to see you manifest the goodness of God.

> Or do you despise the riches of His goodness, forbearance, and longsuffering, not knowing that the goodness of God leads you to repentance?
>
> Romans 2:4 NKJV

Since the goodness of God leads us to repent and turn to God for salvation, our lives ought to preach His goodness to people. How do we do that? If we are making right choices by drawing upon God's grace, then we are showing forth the goodness of the Lord by the way we live our lives. Even when we make a mistake, if we are quick to admit it, apologize, and make things right, we are revealing the power of God's grace in our lives. Such an example says, "Look, I may not always get things right, but my heart's desire is to make the right choice, please God, and love my neighbor. So even when things go wrong, God makes everything work for my good" (see Romans 8:28).

When people are confronted with the goodness of God in our lives again and again, the Holy Spirit has something to work with!

> Nevertheless I tell you the truth; It is expedient for you that I go away: for if I go not away, the Comforter will not come unto you; but if I depart, I will send him unto you.
>
> And when he is come, he will reprove the world of sin, and of righteousness, and of judgment.
>
> John 16:7-8

Jesus said that one of the Holy Spirit's jobs is to convict people of their sins. When someone sees you overcome your sin and do the right thing in the face of all kinds of adversity, the Holy

Spirit can then come in and say, "You see the goodness of God in her life? You could have that too. You could turn away from your life of sin and selfishness and be a part of God's family."

The Bible tells us in Ephesians 2:8 that we are saved by grace. We see the goodness of God and call upon His grace to save us from our sins, from our weaknesses, from our fears, and from eternal death and damnation. But too many Christians stop drawing upon God's grace after salvation. They don't realize that His grace is always there to help them resist temptation and live holy lives. When Christians continue to draw upon God's grace, others see the goodness of God. They see Jesus and want Him too!

Are your family, friends, neighbors, and co-workers seeing the goodness of God in your life? If you are drawing upon His grace to make right choices, and He is adding all you need to succeed in your life, that is a tremendous witness to the grace and goodness of the Lord! Everyone around you will know that the key to your success and happiness is the One you serve.

3

You've 'Gotta Serve Somebody'

In 1979, Bob Dylan released a gospel album, and one of the most famous songs was called, "Gotta Serve Somebody." The main lyric of the song reminds listeners that in life, all of us have to serve somebody. Mr. Dylan states that we may choose to serve the devil or we may choose to serve God, but ultimately, we will serve somebody.

I'm glad Bob Dylan agreed with what the Bible says! In Joshua, chapter 24, Joshua reminded the children of Israel about their history. He spoke of all the things God had done. He brought them out of Egypt. During their wilderness wandering, He was a cloud by day to protect them from the sun and a fire by night to keep them warm in the cold. God gave them victory over their enemies in the Promised Land flowing with milk and honey. Most importantly, God kept all His promises to them.

After recounting all God had done, Joshua gave the Israelites the bottom line:

> Now therefore fear the Lord, and serve him in sincerity and in truth: and put away the gods which your fathers served on the other side of the flood, and in Egypt; and serve ye the Lord.
>
> And if it seem evil unto you to serve the LORD, choose you this day whom ye will serve; whether the gods which your fathers served that were on the other side of the flood, or the gods of the Amorites, in whose land ye dwell: but as for me and my house, we will serve the LORD.
>
> **Joshua 24:14-15**

Joshua was telling the people that they were going to serve somebody, and he wanted them to make the right decision. Just as Israel had a choice then, we have a choice now. Every moment of every day, we choose whether or not we will serve God or someone—or something—else.

In Revelation 3:20, Jesus says, "Behold, I stand at the door, and knock: if any man hear my voice, and open the door, I will come in to him, and will sup with him, and he with me." Jesus knocks at the door of every person's heart, and it's up to each one to choose to let Him in, to hear what He has to say, and to serve Him as Lord and Master—or not.

Romans, chapter 5, says that when Jesus took all our sins on Himself as He died on the cross, He made it possible for you and me to become right with God. He became sin that we might become righteous. When we surrender our lives to Jesus, His Holy Spirit comes to live inside of us and makes us right with God. Righteousness is our new, spiritual condition. Because of one choice—the most important choice a human being can make—we are born again spiritually. Then we have

God's supernatural grace and ability to continue to make right choices for the rest of our lives.

If you have never made Jesus your Lord and Savior, I urge you—I beg you—to do it now. I promise you will never regret it. In fact, you will wish you had done it years ago! You will realize that if you had been serving Jesus instead of whatever or whomever you were serving, you would not have made some of the mistakes you've made or acted certain ways you now regret. He gives you the grace to turn away from evil and do the right thing.

If you are born again, praise the Lord! Now you can explore the depth and breadth of God's love and care for you as you make each decision to serve Him, to seek first His kingdom and His righteousness for the rest of your life.

Looks Can Be Deceiving

There is a way which seemeth right unto a man, but the end thereof are the ways of death.

Proverbs 14:12

If it looks good and feels good to our way of thinking, it must be the right choice. But what we can't see at the moment is where that path will take us and how it will end. We can only view a situation through the information the world and our natural senses gives us. Only God knows the consequences of our choices. Because God is a spirit, we communicate with Him by the Holy Spirit inside us. If we serve the Lord, He can give us information the world and our five natural senses cannot. He can tell us the absolute truth so we can make the right choice.

The Bible reveals that what seems right to us can be very wrong. That ought to make us run to the Father to make sure we are reading the situation correctly. Otherwise, we may experience ruin and heartbreak. You see, there are three fleshly motivations that can get us to go in the wrong direction: lust, greed, and pride. If something gives us pleasure, brings us money, makes us famous or puts us in a great position of authority, you can bet we'll be tempted by it. When I was in my early twenties, I got a call that was so "up my alley" that I didn't even think to ask God about it. At that time, Full Gospel Businessmen chapters were springing up all over America and throughout the world. Back then, the person who led praise and worship at the beginning of a church service was called the song leader. This was something I had done in my church for several years. A member of the board of the Full Gospel Businessmen invited me to travel with them and be their song leader.

I thought, *Wow! This is my big chance.* In my mind, I saw myself singing God's praise to thousands of people at Madison Square Garden, just like George Beverly Shea. I wanted to say, "Yes! I'd love to do it!" But somehow, I managed to tell the man, "I'll pray about it and get back to you."

As I drove to work one morning, I was so excited about this incredible opportunity. I was thinking how I could finally quit my job and travel the world serving the Lord. I thought of all the great places the man told me we would go. Then I heard a still, small voice say, "You haven't asked Me."

I said to the Lord, "But it has to be You! Isn't this You?"

"Better that you preach to the few than that you sing for the thousands."

I wasn't very happy about God's answer. I loved to sing. I was good at leading people in worship. Surely, that was going to be the way God would use me! But deep in my heart, I knew God had called me to preach. Singing and leading worship was a gift He had given me, and He wanted me to use it, but it was not my calling. "Oh, all right," I answered.

Our Father Knows All Things

There's a way that seems right to you and me, but it can often lead to ruin (Proverbs 16:25). This is why we need to seek *God's* righteousness, *His* right choices. Then we can be sure that whatever happens, we are serving Him and not ourselves. If you think this is too hard, remember that Romans 8:28 says that all things work together for our good *when we love the Lord*. Jesus said in John 14:15, "If ye love me, keep my commandments." Loving Jesus is the same as obeying Him. You serve the person you obey, follow, imitate, and admire most.

When we seek first God's righteousness and make the right choice, we are showing how much we love God. Then as we love Him, He works all things together for our good. On the other hand, if we turn away from Him and do our own thing, He has to sit there and watch us make a mess of our lives. Sometimes, these choices can be a matter of life or death.

For if ye live after the flesh, ye shall die: but if ye through the Spirit do mortify the deeds of the body, ye shall live.

For as many as are led by the Spirit of God, they are the sons of God.

Romans 8:13-14

The Bible lays it right on the line: Making the wrong choices can get you killed! The only way you can be sure you are making the right choice is to be led by the Holy Spirit, not your selfish thinking or fleshly desires. God will keep you safe and great things can happen when you are led by Him.

Sometimes being led by the Spirit of God doesn't turn out to be what you thought it would be. God will take good care of you, but you may not get rich and famous or be doing what you thought you'd be doing. The good news is, you will have peace that passes all understanding and the kind of pleasure and accomplishment that will surpass anything you could have imagined or designed for yourself.

Only God knows what will make you happy, because only He knows what's really going on inside you.

> **All the ways of a man are clean in his own eyes; but the Lord weigheth the spirits.**
>
> **Proverbs 16:2**

The word *clean* means pure. This verse is telling us that we may think what we do is clean and pure, but the Lord knows the truth. We may think we have a good reason for doing what we're doing, when really we are completely out of God's will. Now, if we see someone do something wrong, we're quick to call it sinning. Yet, if we do the same thing, we tell ourselves we have a perfectly fine reason for doing the same thing.

It's a good thing we have the Holy Spirit on the inside of us to tell us the truth. "The Lord weigheth the spirits." He sees our true motives, and sometimes those have nothing to do with loving and serving Him. Our "reasons" are nothing more than selfish excuses for getting our way or doing something we want to do that is not God's will.

Whenever we have even the slightest hesitation in our spirits about doing something, we need to put aside all our great reasons for doing it and ask the Lord. We don't want to end up in a ditch tomorrow because we made a wrong turn today.

Jesus Gives Us the Key to Life

In His Sermon on the Mount, Jesus told us the truth about how to live a happy, prosperous life. In Matthew, chapter 6, He began by saying:

Take no thought for your life, what ye shall eat, or what ye shall drink; nor yet for your body, what ye shall put on. Is not the life more than meat, and the body than raiment?

Behold the fowls of the air: for they sow not, neither do they reap, nor gather into barns; yet your heavenly Father feedeth them. Are ye not much better than they?

Which of you by taking thought can add one cubit unto his stature?

And why take ye thought for raiment? Consider the lilies of the field, how they grow; they toil not, neither do they spin:

And yet I say unto you, That even Solomon in all his glory was not arrayed like one of these.

Wherefore, if God so clothe the grass of the field, which to day is, and to morrow is cast into the oven, shall he not much more clothe you, O ye of little faith?

Matthew 6:25-30

Jesus talked about concern for what we wear, what we eat, where we live, and even our stature or reputation. He said that God takes such good care of all His creation, but He takes special care of His own children. We should not be worried about anything! Then Jesus gave us the key to receiving all the blessings God has for us:

> Therefore take no thought, saying, What shall we eat? or, What shall we drink? or, Wherewithal shall we be clothed?
>
> (For after all these things do the Gentiles seek:) for your heavenly Father knoweth that ye have need of all these things.
>
> But seek ye first the kingdom of God, and his righteousness; and all these things shall be added unto you.
>
> Matthew 6:31-33

Your heavenly Father knows what you need and all these things will be given to you. All you need to do is stop worrying and obsessing about what you need and set your eyes and your faith on God. Seek first His kingdom and His righteousness. Make the right choices throughout your day, and let Him surprise you with all kinds of unexpected blessings.

Begin everyday remembering how He loved you so much that He sent Jesus to die for you, how He forgave you and gave you a brand-new life, and how He is greater than any problem or trouble you are facing at this moment. Isn't it a privilege, honor, and joy to serve Him?

You notice in Matthew 6:33 that Jesus mentioned seeking the kingdom of God before seeking His righteousness. What does that mean? He explained this in detail to Nicodemus in John, chapter 3.

> Jesus answered and said unto him, Verily, verily, I say unto thee, Except a man be born again, he cannot see the kingdom of God.

Nicodemus saith unto him, How can a man be born when he is old? can he enter the second time into his mother's womb, and be born?

Jesus answered, Verily, verily, I say unto thee, Except a man be born of water and of the Spirit, he cannot enter into the kingdom of God.

That which is born of the flesh is flesh; and that which is born of the Spirit is spirit.

Marvel not that I said unto thee, Ye must be born again.

The wind bloweth where it listeth, and thou hearest the sound thereof, but canst not tell whence it cometh, and whither it goeth: so is every one that is born of the Spirit.

John 3:3-8

Jesus said that only by being born again, spiritually regenerated by the Holy Spirit, can you *see* and *enter* the kingdom of God. You cannot understand and be a part of God's kingdom unless you have His Spirit living inside you. In verse 5, He went on to say that He was not talking about a second natural birth; He was talking about a spiritual rebirth. To enter the kingdom and to understand the kingdom, your spirit must be born again by the Holy Spirit.

Adam and Eve were filled with the Holy Spirit, but they sinned and He had to leave them. All of us are descended from Adam and Eve, so we are born spiritually dead or separated from God and His eternal life. Through Jesus we can be "born again" spiritually. When we receive Jesus as our Lord and Savior, the Holy Spirit comes into our dead spirits, makes us alive again to God, and we have eternal life. Hallelujah! Jesus is the key to eternal life, and serving Him is the key to living life to the fullest.

We Serve the Greatest!

A person becomes righteous, or has right standing with God, the moment they are born again. Even in those first moments, you know you are fundamentally different than you were before you received Jesus as your Lord and Savior. You are a new creation! You have an intimate relationship with the Father, Jesus, and the Holy Spirit on the inside of you. It is utterly miraculous!

What I have just described is your *position* of being righteous in Christ Jesus. That happens when you are born again, and you didn't have anything to do with it. You didn't earn it, win it, or persuade God to give it to you. You simply put your faith in Jesus Christ to redeem you from sin and be the Lord of your life. The Holy Spirit entered your dead spirit, spiritually joined you to the Father, and began to urge you to seek the kingdom and His righteousness. Now and for as long as you live, the Holy Spirit will enable you to manifest God's kingdom and His righteousness in the way you live your life. All you have to do is love and serve the greatest one who ever walked the earth—Jesus.

When all that God promises us does not come to pass, sometimes it is because we're not walking in concert with Him. We've swerved off the path of righteousness and are serving ourselves, someone else, or something else. Christians can know they are righteous and part of God's kingdom and still not make the right choices. God's design is that we work out our salvation with fear and trembling (Philippians 2:12). Some right choices can't be made any other way! There are some things I never would have done right if I didn't fear God and tremble at His Word.

Jesus wouldn't have said to seek both the kingdom and His righteousness if just getting into the kingdom of God was all He was after. He also encouraged us to seek His righteousness or

His right choices. Jesus doesn't want only to be your Savior; He also wants to be the Lord of your life. Then He can bless you! When you serve Him and Him alone, "all these things shall be added unto you."

Today, Jesus might have said it this way: "When you're walking with Me and making right choices, I will bless you with everything you need in life. Because you have been born again and are choosing to serve Me in everything you think, say, and do, I will add to your life everything you need."

In Matthew 6:33, Jesus gave us a vital key to experiencing answered prayers and a happy, prosperous life: seek God's kingdom and His righteousness. Jesus made us righteous by shedding His innocent blood on the cross at Calvary. His Spirit and His mighty Word enable us to make right choices that honor Him.

When you serve the Lord with all your heart, soul, mind, and strength, you demonstrate His righteousness and the glory of His kingdom to everyone you meet.

4

Let Jesus Shine

Your life in Jesus Christ is like a lighthouse, a shining city on a hill. Let everybody look and see what a joy it is to serve Him! He will bless you, He will keep you, He will heal you, and He will supply your needs. He will bless your children and your children's children. And the best part is, the world will see Him shining through your life.

We have a responsibility to show everyone we meet the real Jesus. The devil, the world, and our flesh work overtime to show people who Jesus is not. He's not sinning, selfish, grumbling, groping in the dark, and grasping at straws. He's full of love, faith, peace, joy, and all the wisdom and strength we need to navigate this wicked, complicated world. He is the Way, the Truth, and the Life (John 14:6), and our lives should reflect Him as the moon reflects the sun.

Letting Jesus shine through us is not always easy, especially because we have an enemy who loves to harass us. (I think his specialty is messing with my computer!) I hate it when I realize

I've opened a door for him to get to me or someone else because I've made a wrong choice. When that happens, I'm quick to repent and slam the door in the enemy's face. Most of the time, he harasses me just because I love and serve the Lord. His entire focus is to stop me from letting Jesus shine through me.

I was driving to a church in Detroit where I was going to preach on a Sunday morning. As I was going over an overpass, I heard a loud noise, my car swerved, and I realized one of my tires had blown. There I was, alone, dressed in my nice, white, preaching suit. I got out and carefully looked around as trucks and cars flew by. Traffic was going too fast for anyone to stop and help me, so I put on my overcoat and raised the trunk, acting like I knew what I was doing.

I managed to get the spare tire and the jack out of the trunk, and I remembered how my daddy showed me to operate the jack and raise the car. Once the car was raised, I tried and tried, but I could not get the blown tire off. Those nuts would not budge. This was typical harassment from the enemy, and I knew it!

At that moment, the Lord spoke this verse of scripture to my heart: "The joy of the Lord is your strength," (Nehemiah 8:10). Right there on Sunday morning in broad daylight, I stood straight up on that busy overpass and raised my hands to Heaven, shouting, "Hallelujah! Glory to God! Thank You, Jesus!"

When the enemy came to kill, steal, and destroy what I was doing for the Lord, I made the right choice. I drew strength from the God who has unlimited power and might. I got happy, and I unscrewed those nuts and had that spare tire on in no time. I got to church with my white suit still white, and I preached to the glory of God.

When you're harassed, keep going! Having problems and feeling like nothing is going right doesn't mean God has left you. It means you have an opportunity to seek His righteousness and be blessed. Jesus said in Matthew 5:10, "Blessed are they which are persecuted for righteousness' sake: for theirs is the kingdom of heaven." Satan is harassing you because of who you are and what you have. When you make the right choices in the midst of the attack, God will bless you with everything you need. And through it all, you will bless others by showing them how Jesus is the Way, the Truth, and the Life in a difficult situation.

Jesus Delivers

Riches profit not in the day of wrath: but righteousness delivereth from death.

The righteousness of the perfect shall direct his way: but the wicked shall fall by his own wickedness.

Proverbs 11:4-5

Perfect in this context means mature. Mature believers seek God's kingdom and His righteousness first, so they have His grace to make the right choices. The righteousness of Jesus Christ in you not only empowers you to think, speak, and act correctly, but also those choices allow Jesus to deliver you from death in all its forms. He will deliver you from sin, from sickness, from poverty, from loneliness and anything ungodly in your life.

Making the right choices will get you out of trouble and keep you out of trouble. Other times, you may be doing nothing wrong, but find yourself in a difficult situation. The Holy Spirit may have led you there for God's purposes and His glory. Sometimes trouble comes because the enemy is on the attack against your good testimony. One choice that will keep you out of financial trouble is the decision to give tithes and offerings. Too many Christians are completely uptight about this, resenting those preachers who tell them if they don't tithe, their tires will blow and their money will leak through cracks in their bank account. When I was on the way to Detroit, my tire blew and I had to pay to get it fixed, but it had nothing to do with a failure to tithe. I'm a tither! This was an example of something happening simply because the enemy was up to no good. But I will tell you that being a tither gives you confidence that Jesus will deliver you when the enemy shows up.

I've always been a tither, and God has always taken good care of me. Tithing should not be a sore spot for us. Jesus gave it all for us, so we should want to give it all for Him. Giving in any way, whether it's our tithe, an offering, or a helping hand, should be a joy to us because in giving, we are serving the Lord and letting Him shine through us.

When we got married, Brother John earned fifty dollars a week. He told me, "Anne, I don't think we can afford to tithe."

I said, "John, I don't think we can afford not to tithe. We'll tithe our way out of this. We'll give and we'll give and we'll get out of it." It wasn't too long before we were giving much more than ten percent!

The righteousness of the upright shall deliver them: but transgressors shall be taken in their own naughtiness.

The righteous is delivered out of trouble, and the wicked cometh in his stead.

Proverbs 11:6, 8

When you stumble into trouble or if the Holy Spirit leads you into trouble, just follow His lead and watch Jesus deliver you in, through, and out of that trouble. The important choices always begin with the perfect, mature decision to call upon the Lord, hear Him, and obey Him. Then, when you are delivered, He gets all the glory! After all these years, I can tell you with confidence that the righteousness of the Upright (His name is Jesus) shall deliver you. All you have to do is make the right choice, the Bible choice, the God choice.

Right choices deliver you from the trouble of worry, distress, and anxiety. You have no reason to be concerned about your safety or well-being when Jesus is at the center of every choice you are making. Even if unexpected trouble arises, His Word assures you that you have all the power of Heaven to deliver you.

This truth applies to cities as well.

When it goeth well with the righteous, the city rejoiceth: and when the wicked perish, there is shouting.

By the blessing of the upright the city is exalted: but it is overthrown by the mouth of the wicked.

Proverbs 11:10-11

A city rejoices and is prosperous and safe when the righteous thrive. When believers make right choices, the presence of God is welcomed into the city in which they live. God can bless a nation that has a church that's alive and full of people seeking first His kingdom and His righteousness.

Jesus wants to shine through cities and nations, but He cannot do that unless His Church seeks first His kingdom and His righteousness. When each of us make right choices, then Jesus can shine through His body and the world will sit up and take notice. Remember, He said that if He is lifted up, then He will draw all people to Himself (John 12:32). Every time we make a right decision, we exalt Jesus in this world.

Even our prayers bring God's glory to this earth:

I exhort therefore, that, first of all, supplications, prayers, intercessions, and giving of thanks, be made for all men;

For kings, and for all that are in authority; that we may lead a quiet and peaceable life in all godliness and honesty.

For this is good and acceptable in the sight of God our Saviour;

Who will have all men to be saved, and to come unto the knowledge of the truth.

1 Timothy 2:1-4

We should always pray for people to be saved, especially those who hold offices of authority. Pray for those in authority to receive Jesus as their Lord and Savior, and if they already have, pray for them to walk in His wisdom and grace. The more the righteous act righteously, the more Jesus can deliver their cities and nations. Then the people will prosper and rejoice. While the future settlers of Massachusetts Bay Colony were still on board their ship, the great Puritan preacher, John Winthrop, admonished them that they would be "as a city set upon a hill." The whole world would be watching them. He was referring to Jesus' admonition from the Sermon on the Mount:

Ye are the light of the world. A city that is set on an hill cannot be hid.

Matthew 5:14

The first settlers and founders of America made some wrong choices, but the majority of their choices were right. That's why our nation has had a tremendous impact for God on the rest of the world—so far. It's up to our generation and future generations of believers to remember Jesus' words and be that heavenly light that shines and dispels the darkness around us. We want our nation to rejoice!

What Dims Your Light?

The wicked worketh a deceitful work: but to him that soweth righteousness shall be a sure reward.

Proverbs 11:18

Do you know that everything you say and do either shines the light of Jesus into the lives of those around you or confuses their understanding of who He is? If you are truly a believer in Jesus Christ, born again and filled with His Spirit, then you represent Him wherever you go.

When you say or do something mean to a person who knows you are a Christian, you are giving them the wrong impression of who Jesus is. On the other hand, if you say something kind and encouraging, that person is going to feel Jesus' loving presence by just being around you. Your right choices lift Him up, so He can draw others to Himself.

Sometimes we know our light is dim because of what comes back at us after we say or do something. We learn to change the way we talk to or about people by how we feel inside afterwards. When something we do comes back to haunt us, we are motivated to stop sinning and walk in a way that pleases the Lord.

The light of Jesus should shine even in the way we *think* about other people! After all, Jesus said what is in our hearts counts.

Blessed are the pure in heart: for they shall see God.

Matthew 5:8

But I say unto you, That whosoever looketh on a woman to lust after her hath committed adultery with her already in his heart.

Matthew 5:28

For where your treasure is, there will your heart be also.

Matthew 6:21

Out of the abundance of the heart the mouth speaketh.

A good man out of the good treasure of the heart bringeth forth good things: and an evil man out of the evil treasure bringeth forth evil things.

Matthew 12:34-35

If Jesus is living in our hearts, we should be thinking like Him, talking like Him, and doing the works that He did. If we feel an uneasy tug in our spirit, we should close our mouth in mid-sentence or stop what we are doing and make a correction. We don't want our lights to be dimmed by something in our hearts that is not right.

It's hard to be a shining light for Jesus Christ if you think like the world, talk trash, and act like God doesn't exist. People not only see your actions, but also see the consequences of your actions—more trouble and misery! On the other hand, if you are making right choices, people can see how God loves you and blesses you. That is when the lights come on, and they can see Jesus.

The Next Generation

Just as we either let Jesus shine through us to the people in our lives or hide Him from them, we also either hide or reveal Him to our children, grandchildren, and maybe even great-grandchildren.

As righteousness tendeth to life: so he that pursueth evil pursueth it to his own death.

The fruit of the righteous is a tree of life; and he that winneth souls is wise.

Proverbs 11:19, 30

Righteousness brings life—the heavenly, eternal, God-kind of life. In John 10:10, Jesus called it abundant life. Right choices will bring you into a life greater than you could ever dream of having, and God's everlasting life will flow through you to your children and your children's children.

I wrote a book about how you mark your children for God. Your children learn more from watching you make right choices than they do when you tell them what is right. Most likely, they will have to reap the consequences of some wrong choices to see that life is much better when they make right choices, but hopefully they will have your godly example and instruction to lead them and guide them.

When your children see you make a choice that is difficult, maybe because of persecution or maybe because your flesh wants to go a different direction, they see Jesus working in your life. They see you drawing upon His courage and grace to do the right thing. They sense His loving, peaceful presence after you make the right choice. They also see how He blesses you as a result of your obedience to Him. Your children will see Jesus in you and want Him in their lives too, bringing them eternal life.

Flourishing in the Lord

Proverbs 11:28 says, "He that trusteth in his riches shall fall; but the righteous (those making right choices) shall flourish (succeed, thrive, grow, increase, prosper, bloom) as a branch" (explanations mine). How could the people in your life not notice when Jesus brings such blessing into your life? If we are not flourishing in Him, it's probably because we didn't check our hearts and thoughts, said the wrong thing, or did something we shouldn't have done. We made the wrong choice, and that cut off the flow of His blessings.

Now I'm not just talking about financial blessings. I'm talking about blessings in every area, especially in our relationships. Proverbs 16:7 says, "When a man's ways please the LORD, he maketh even his enemies to be at peace with him." Wow! I want my ways to please the Lord! What a blessing, to have my enemies be at peace with me, with my city, and with my nation.

When would a person's ways please the Lord? When the person prayed and made the right choice. When he or she acted righteously by doing the right thing in God's will. Psalm 37:23 says that the steps of a good or righteous person are ordered by the Lord, and that person delights in doing His will. Those who please the Lord don't take joy in what society says is politically correct or what will keep their neighbors from talking about them. They delight in doing things God's way.

Sometimes we just sit in church and endure being Christians. We don't want to go to hell, and we don't want to be bad people, so we just keep trying to be good little Christians. But we aren't happy! I get like that when I forget to let Jesus shine through me. Because I'm in the ministry, when I'm with others I am always aware that I need to make right choices. But when I'm by myself, and no one's watching, I can slip.

If I don't read and study my Bible, I get away from the truth. I forget who I am and what I'm supposed to be doing. I stop listening to the Holy Spirit and allow the enemy to rob me of the true joy and pleasure that only comes from letting Jesus shine through me. And all this can happen in my living room when I'm by myself! I've learned that Jesus wants to shine through me, even when I'm the only one who knows it.

I delight to do thy will, O my God: yea, thy law is within my heart.

Psalm 40:8

You've got the Word of God and the Spirit of God working inside you to show you what God's will is for your life, and that alone should make you happy. If you are bored, tired, and wondering what happened to all that zeal you used to have, you need to make some right choices. Go to the Word of God, make sure you get a full meal, and then chew on it until you fall asleep that night. Let Jesus wash you, give you revelation, and inspire you to do mighty exploits. Let Him shine!

If you're enduring every church service, ask God if you're in the right church. That's one of the most important choices you make. If He says, "You're right where I want you," then *you* are the problem! You need to stir up your gifts and get involved where you will take delight in doing His will. If He says, "I've called you to learn, grow, and serve over there, with that other congregation," then tell your pastor you made a mistake and go introduce yourself to the pastor and congregation God pointed you to.

You must come to the conclusion that if nobody else chooses to go on with God, you're going! Don't even look back to see if you have a train behind you. You just go with Him and let Him shine.

You can make a choice for Jesus because Jesus made a choice for you. Thank God, He sweat blood in the Garden of Gethsemane, considered the joy of you, and said, "Father, not My will, but Yours be done" (see Luke 22:42). He made the right choice and sowed a seed of righteousness that had your name on it! Now you have the privilege and honor of making the right choice to let Jesus shine through you.

5

....

Praying with Confidence

One of the challenges I have faced over the years in my walk with the Lord is having confidence that when I pray, God hears me and is answering me. Well, no more! The revelation of righteousness that God is giving me has completely changed my understanding of how we can pray with confidence.

> **For the eyes of the Lord are over the righteous, and his ears are open unto their prayers: but the face of the Lord is against them that do evil.**
>
> **1 Peter 3:12**

I want you to notice something. The Word of God doesn't say that the face of the Lord is against those who are not born again; it says He is against those who do evil. The last part of this verse is not talking about our spiritual condition; it is talking about our actions once we are born again. The Lord expects those He has made righteous through His blood to act like it. In fact, He cannot answer the prayers of those who choose not to follow Him and do evil.

A lot of Christians are praying, but many of their prayers don't go higher than the ceiling. The only prayers God hears are those that come from the lips of people who seek first His kingdom and His righteousness, who are not only righteous in Him but also act like it. They are truly submitted to Him as the Lord of their lives and are making godly choices. Therefore, God hears them and answers their prayers.

Just as the eyes of the Lord are upon believers who make right choices, His face is against or turned away from those who do evil. Doing evil isn't just committing murder, stealing, or having sex outside of marriage. Yes, that's evil, but doing evil includes anything that is outside the will of God. It's choosing your way over God's way. Anything that is not God's will is a selfish and oftentimes immoral, destructive, depraved choice.

You can't be watching pornography, hitting your spouse, or cheating on tests at school and expect God to hear your prayers. The only prayer He will hear from you is, "Forgive me, Father! I repent and turn away from this sin." As soon as you honor Him and make the right choice to turn back to Him, He will hear you and give you all the help you need to keep making the right choices.

Some believers misuse God's grace and their position of being righteous. They believe they can live any way they want and God still will hear their prayers. They say, "I have prosperity because I am righteous in Christ Jesus," but they don't tithe, help others, or pay their bills on time. When God doesn't answer their prayer to enable them to buy a house or car, they blame Him instead of searching the Word and asking the Holy Spirit to show them where they missed it.

Thriving Christians obey 1 Thessalonians 5:17 and pray without ceasing. Prayer is like breathing to them. They are always communicating with their King. They listen to Him when He speaks to them. Because they are seeking first His righteousness, they have complete confidence in their prayers.

People tell me they've prayed to God about something, but then they say, "Well, I hope He heard me. I just pray He answers." They have no confidence God heard their prayer! They feel compelled to pray the same prayer over and over because they're not sure God heard them. They might be ignorant of what God's Word promises them, or they might be making wrong choices and failing to seek God first in all things. Either way, they have no confidence or faith in their prayers.

Do you have confidence when you pray? Do you know God hears you and answers you? If you don't, maybe it is because you have not been seeking the kingdom of God by serving your King and seeking His righteousness by doing His will.

For our proud confidence is this: the testimony of our conscience, that in holiness and godly sincerity, not in fleshly wisdom but in the grace of God, we have conducted ourselves in the world, and especially toward you.

2 Corinthians 1:12 NASB

You will have confidence in your prayers when your conscience is clear, knowing you have made godly choices and sought the Lord and His grace in all things.

Proof of the Kingdom

Every kingdom has a king and in the kingdom of God, Jesus is our King. He was brought forth by God through the Jewish people, so He is also the Jewish Messiah. His Jewish cousin, John the Baptist, was probably the first to realize this. He was thrown into prison for his fiery preaching declaring the arrival of the Promised One. But after John had been in prison a while, he got discouraged and sent a couple of his disciples to ask Jesus if He was truly the Messiah.

> Now when John had heard in the prison the works of Christ, he sent two of his disciples,
>
> and said unto him, Art thou he that should come, or do we look for another?
>
> Jesus answered and said unto them, Go and shew John again those things which ye do hear and see:
>
> The blind receive their sight, and the lame walk, the lepers are cleansed, and the deaf hear, the dead are raised up, and the poor have the gospel preached to them.
>
> And blessed is he, whosoever shall not be offended in me.
>
> Matthew 11:2-6

Jesus walked this earth and miracles happened like it was normal. He proved that He was the Messiah by His works, and every work He listed for John the Baptist was supernatural. Of course, the greatest miracle a human being can experience is receiving Jesus as Lord and Savior. That's why Jesus said, "Blessed is he, whosoever shall not be offended in me."

When Jesus said, "Tell John what you've seen, what you've heard, and what is happening," He was saying, "Tell him the kingdom of God is here because miracles are happening. The enemy is being displaced, literally kicked out of people's lives. Their minds, hearts, and bodies are being divinely touched and transformed. The Messiah has come to put things right!"

Isn't this exciting? We are to seek first God's kingdom, where our King is all-powerful, all-knowing, and all-present! Because the kingdom of God is here in us right now, we should have no trouble praying for the sick and expecting them to be made well, praying for the demon-possessed and expecting them to be freed, and praying for opportunities to lead people to the Lord and expecting them to be saved. In all this, we should have no trouble drawing upon God's grace to make the right choices.

If we're not seeing the works of Jesus in our lives, in our churches, and in the lives of believers we know, then something is amiss. We are not seeking the kingdom of God and His righteousness. The kingdom should manifest for us in the same way the kingdom manifested for Jesus when He walked the earth.

Jesus Is Our Model

Verily, verily, I say unto you, He that believeth on me, the works that I do shall he do also; and greater works than these shall he do; because I go unto my Father.

John 14:12

Jesus said that we would do the works He did. If we follow Him, we should see some spectacular things happen! We need to begin where He always began—in prayer. Jesus always prayed before He spoke or did anything. He said that He never did anything He didn't first see His Father doing.

Then answered Jesus and said unto them, Verily, verily, I say unto you, The Son can do nothing of himself, but what he seeth the Father do: for what things soever he doeth, these also doeth the Son likewise.

John 5:19

Jesus said a lot about our Father in Heaven. He said that seeing and knowing Him (Jesus) is seeing and knowing the Father. We can have this confidence, that our Father wants to heal everyone who's sick, just like Jesus did; He wants to deliver everyone who's oppressed or possessed of the devil, just like Jesus did; and He wants to save every man, woman, and child on this earth, which is why Jesus died.

And it came to pass, that, as he was praying in a certain place, when he ceased, one of his disciples said unto him, Lord, teach us to pray, as John also taught his disciples.

And he said unto them, When ye pray, say, Our Father which art in heaven, Hallowed be thy name. Thy kingdom come. Thy will be done, as in heaven, so in earth.

Luke 11:1-2

Jesus taught us to pray, "Thy kingdom come. Thy will be done." Sounds a lot like "seek His kingdom and His righteousness," doesn't it? We are to begin our prayers by going directly to the Father in Jesus' name. Our first right choice is to go to the Father in prayer. Our second right choice is to pray correctly.

And this is the confidence that we have in him, that, if we ask any thing according to his will, he heareth us:

And if we know that he hear us, whatsoever we ask, we know that we have the petitions that we desired of him.

1 John 5:14-15

We must choose to pray according to God's will, which we can find in His Word and know by His Spirit. The most powerful prayers we pray, the ones God always hears, are His own Word. The Word builds our faith when we pray. Romans 10:17 tells us that faith comes and grows strong by hearing over and over again the Word of God. Long before Jesus ever prayed for the sick or preached to the multitudes here on earth, He spent years studying the scrolls of Scriptures and talking with the rabbis in the synagogues and in the Temple. He is our example.

As we study God's Word, the Holy Spirit teaches us, guides us, comforts us, instructs us, and sometimes rebukes and corrects us. Jesus sent Him to us for this purpose (John 14:16-18). When we pray in the Spirit and read and study God's Word, the Holy Spirit lets us know that we are hearing directly from the Father. God is speaking to us! And when you hear a word from God, your faith and your confidence in what you pray soars!

Jesus called the Holy Spirit "the Spirit of *truth*." He will tell us exactly what to pray because He knows God's will in all situations. He will tell us the absolute truth. Sometimes we like what He tells us and sometimes we don't, but if we pray according to God's will, according to what the Spirit has spoken directly to our hearts, we can pray in faith and confidence, knowing God heard us and will answer us. Even if our natural thinking and emotions don't like what we're praying, we will have His peace and grace that we have made the right choice in praying His will, not ours.

Jesus always prayed by the Spirit according to God's will and Word. That's why He could stand in front of His friend Lazarus' tomb and declare,

Father, I thank thee that thou hast heard me.

And I knew that thou hearest me always: but because of the people which stand by I said it, that they may believe that thou hast sent me.

And when he thus had spoken, he cried with a loud voice, Lazarus, come forth.

And he that was dead came forth, bound hand and foot with graveclothes: and his face was bound about with a napkin. Jesus saith unto them, Loose him, and let him go.

John 11:41-44

Jesus yelled, "Lazarus, come forth," and out came Lazarus, raised from the dead and fully healed. How did this happen? Jesus prayed in faith and full confidence that His Father heard Him and would answer His prayer. You might say, "Well, of course! He's the King of the kingdom. He's the Son of God, so naturally everything He prays comes to pass." Jesus may be the Son of God, but He is also "the firstborn of many brethren" (Romans 8:29). That means He is our Elder Brother, and we are to be like Him and do His works. We have no excuses! We must make right choices, and that includes praying God's will with confidence, just like Jesus did.

Do Good to Pray Good

If I am seeking God on a particular matter, He often speaks to me through the New Testament epistles. They are filled with His wisdom to build my faith and open my mind and heart to revelation about who He is, who I am, what I'm to be doing, what the Church is to be doing, and what I should be praying.

Sometimes the Holy Spirit has to do some housecleaning in me before I can pray.

When couples come to me for counsel, the Holy Spirit often leads me to 1 Peter 3:7:

> Likewise, ye husbands, dwell with them according to knowledge, giving honour unto the wife, as unto the weaker vessel, and as being heirs together of the grace of life; that your prayers be not hindered.

Here we see clearly that how we treat other people can directly affect whether or not our prayers are answered. A husband who doesn't spend time with his wife to get to know her, doesn't show her honor and respect, forgets that she may not be as physically strong as he is, and doesn't treat her as a sister in the Lord who is loved and cherished by God—that man is not going to get his prayers answered.

This is an incredibly important scripture for husbands. Any man who is about to get married needs to understand that this is what God expects of him. These are the right choices he must make toward his wife if he wants to pray confidently and know that God hears him and will answer him.

This scripture tells all of us that we need to make right choices—especially toward others—if we want God to hear our prayers. The apostle John wrote, "If we walk in the light, as he is in the light, we have fellowship one with another" (1 John 1:7). It's hard to have fellowship with someone you haven't forgiven or haven't treated right. You're not walking in the light of God's Word and His Spirit.

Psalm 119:105 says, "Thy word is a lamp unto my feet, and a light unto my path." We have come full circle: The Word and the Spirit show us how to pray and what to do. As we do the right thing, we treat others right, and then we can pray with confidence.

When I'm making right choices in fellowship with God, I have no hesitation in my prayers. I come boldly to the throne of grace and know God hears me because I'm coming in faith in His Word, I'm full of His Spirit, and there's nothing in my heart that tells me I've got something that I need to get right first.

You can't go to God and pray confidently if you have sin in your life. The best thing to do is not to sin in the first place! That's why Jesus sent the Holy Spirit and gave us His Word, so we would have His supernatural ability and grace to resist temptation and do the right thing. But if you have sinned, repent and pray for courage and perseverance to overcome that sin completely.

One day I was in a drug store where I knew I could buy some stamps. The machine was at the back of the store, where hardly anyone went. I put the money in the machine and turned the knob to release the stamps, and that machine started spitting out little boxes of stamps all over the place. I couldn't believe what I was seeing! Blessings were falling out of Heaven!

But then I came to my senses. Those stamps were not coming from God; they were coming out of a broken stamp machine, and I had a choice to make. No one was around. No one was looking. I could take all those stamps and no one would know. Except Jesus.

I gathered up the boxes and went immediately to the druggist. I said, "I need to tell you that your stamp machine is spitting these things out over there."

He said, "Oh! Thank you. You keep 'em. Thank you for telling me!"

Only after I made the right choice were those stamps a gift from Heaven! If I had not overcome the temptation to sneak off with the stamps, I would have been stealing from that man and his store and my stomach would have churned until I made it right. Hear this: There is no wrong choice or sin that is worth losing your peace with God! Don't cheat. Don't steal. Don't lie. Don't curse. "Oh it just slipped." Well, quit letting it slip! It's a choice you make, and God sees and knows everything. You want to always go to Him with clean lips, a clean heart, and a clean slate. Then you can be certain that He hears your prayers.

> **My little children, these things write I unto you, that ye sin not. And if any man sin, we have an advocate with the Father, Jesus Christ the righteous:**
>
> **And he is the propitiation for our sins: and not for ours only, but also for the sins of the whole world.**
>
> **And hereby we do know that we know him, if we keep his commandments.**
>
> **1 John 2:1-3**

John urges us not to sin, to make right choices. When we do sin, repent, and receive forgiveness, we must remember what our forgiveness cost Jesus. If we look at the cross, we will think twice before sinning again! John goes on to say that we can only really know Jesus by keeping His commandments, by making right choices. I don't know about you, but I want to know Him!

One of the reasons Jesus prayed with such confidence was because He was without sin. Making right choices and refusing to sin is one of the greatest of His works that we can do in this life. Then we can pray in confidence like He does.

Heartfelt Prayers

A clear conscience is what we need whenever we come to the Father in prayer, but we also need to allow the Word and the Spirit to examine our hearts, to reveal our true motives. We want to be sure we're not so centered on what we think we need and want that we miss what God is trying to do at that moment.

We also need to go to the Word and listen to the Holy Spirit because sometimes we need to be brought back to earth with some good old common sense.

When my daughter Robin was little, I taught her what I call the "Nevertheless Prayer." Sometimes children will pray for the craziest things, so I taught Robin to pray, "Nevertheless Father, not my will but Thine be done." I was training her to make right choices, to pray in faith and trust God for the result.

One day Robin lost a ring that her daddy and I had given her. That night, when I tucked her in bed, she was so upset because she couldn't find the ring. She said, "Mother, please pray that I'll find it." She was so devastated, but she made the right choice and turned to God.

I said, "Let's pray right now," and knelt down beside her bed. She had one of those shaggy rugs in her room. As I knelt, I felt something digging into me and said, "What in the world is this?" It was the ring! You just never know how quickly your prayers are going to get answered, and you can never underestimate the fervent prayer of a little child.

In Psalm 120:1, David said, "In my distress I cried unto the LORD, and he heard me." David committed some grievous sins in his adult life, but he was quick to repent. He had a heart for God before anything else. Whenever he was in trouble (and he experienced a lot of it), he always looked to God and God was there for him.

We don't want God to turn away from us in time of trouble. We want His eyes to be on us and His ears open to our cry. To avoid crazy, selfish prayers and keep our hearts and minds stayed on the Lord, there is nothing like a good old time of confession. James tells us:

> Confess your faults one to another, and pray one for another, that ye may be healed. The effectual fervent prayer of a righteous man availeth much.

> **James 5:16**

The *Amplified Bible* says it like this:

> Therefore, confess your sins to one another [your false steps, your offenses], and pray for one another, that you may be healed *and* restored. The heartfelt *and* persistent prayer of a righteous man (believer) can accomplish much [when put into action and made effective by God—it is dynamic and can have tremendous power].

God hears your prayers when you make right choices and pray from the very core of your being, laying it all on the line for Him. He sees that you're full of faith, standing on His Word, following His Spirit, and completely confident—just like Jesus.

> Cast not away therefore your confidence, which hath great recompence of reward.

> **Hebrews 10:35**

Don't cast away your confidence by making the wrong choices! Always remember that walking with the Lord in His will, His way, and His right choices, makes your prayers powerful. God will move mountains on your behalf. Your prayers, prayed in faith and with nothing wrong between you and the Lord, can change the atmosphere around you and bring God's blessings down from Heaven.

6

....

What Brings the Blessings of God?

Our God is a good God. All you have to do is look around at His beautiful creation to see how much He wants to bless us. And if that's not good enough for you, just look at the cross. God sent His only Son to die for your sins. Jesus died so you could BE righteous and then ACT righteous. Being righteous means you have His supernatural ability to always make right choices. In His amazing grace, you can decide things according to His Word as His Spirit leads you.

People who haven't experienced this miracle that Jesus calls being born again may ask, "What's the point? My life is fine. Why would I want to be right with God, anyway?"

I have a lot of answers for that! Here are the top five:

• You know you're going to Heaven when you die.

• You know your sins are forgiven—past, present, and future.

- You can get to know the God who created the universe on very intimate terms as your real Father.

- Your personal relationship with God reveals who you really are and your divine purpose.

- You will be supernaturally empowered by God to be the person you were created to be and do everything you were created to do.

Unless you are one of those people who never wants to make a decision for yourself, you'll appreciate another big reason God is a good God: He gave you the power to choose. He respects your choices, which doesn't mean He will agree with them, but He respects your right to choose. He gave you freedom of choice. You are a free moral agent. That means your life consists of the rewards or consequences of your decisions.

Even a baby can like or dislike different foods. They will spit out what they don't like. We can try to force them to eat their vegetables (what a mess!), but eventually they will grow up and choose whether or not they will eat them.

We dress children when they're little, but as they grow older, they want to choose their own clothes. Adolescents begin dating, and we do our best to steer them in the right direction. As young adults, they bring home someone they want to marry. We do our best to pray and influence our child to marry God's choice, but we can't pick their mate. We just have to pray we taught them to seek God's kingdom and His righteousness above all else. Being a parent gives you a new respect for our heavenly Father and His goodness!

You might be saying, "Well, I grew up in poverty and was terribly abused, and I sure didn't choose that. What did I know about making my own choices? I was a kid! Where was God in that?"

Many times the people who are close to us choose to do terrible things to us, but God had nothing to do with their wrong choices. If those people who hurt you had been listening to God, they would have treated you differently. But just like all of us, they had the power to make their own choices and their choices hurt you. But that was your past; now you are reading the truth. You can change your life by taking responsibility for your decisions and charting a new course for your life.

Taking responsibility for your choices, even the little ones you don't give much thought to, will change your life. On some level, even as kids, we make our own choices. We choose to obey or not, which means we choose the consequences of our actions. When things happen to us, we choose how we will respond. We decide whether or not we will use our experiences to motivate us to do good or evil.

You decide if you'll go to school or skip it. You decide if you'll finish high school and go to college or go to work. You decide if you'll take a certain job. It's your choice whether or not to do drugs, have sex outside of marriage, or steal to get what you need and want. You make a conscious decision.

Many times, there are tremendous pressures to get you to choose a certain thing or course of action, but ultimately it is your decision. If you are a Christian, the world, the devil, and your flesh will try to compel you to make wrong choices. But God's Word, the Holy Spirit, your brothers and sisters in the Lord, and your pastor, are encouraging you to make right choices. They want you to have a good life, and they know that won't happen if you make bad decisions.

The Power of One Choice

For just a moment, I want you to imagine standing by a beautiful, clear-blue lake. You pick up a small pebble and throw it into that lake. Not only will you see ripples moving out from the place your pebble landed, but for longer than you'll ever know or see, there will be vibrations underneath the water that affect the depth and breadth of that lake and anyone or anything in it or on it. This is the power of one choice!

When I was sixteen years old, I received Jesus Christ and was filled with the Holy Spirit in a tent meeting in Corpus Christi, Texas. That decision not only changed my life, but also it changed the lives of everyone I knew. Some were happy for me, and some were not, but I had definitely thrown my pebble into the lake!

My decision to follow Christ affected my parents' lives and my sister's life. It determined who I married, how we raised our daughter, and how we love and treat our grandchildren. That one decision directed my life's work, where I would live, and what I would do there. I won't know until I get to Heaven all the ramifications of choosing Jesus as my Lord and Savior, but it is the one decision that affects everything in life.

Being born again is the most important decision anyone can make. Jesus said: "Seek ye FIRST the kingdom of God, and his righteousness," (Matthew 6:33, emphasis mine). When you receive Jesus Christ into your heart and give Him your life, do you know what you receive in return? You get the kingdom of God. You know the King of kings and the Lord of lords, and you enter a spiritual dimension where He is involved in everything that affects your life.

Countless blessings flow in as you walk with the Lord, and countless blessings flow out as you do His will and bless others.

Of course, if you make wrong choices and take your life into your own hands, the blessings dwindle away. When you shut Jesus out and ignore Him, He will try to get your attention for a while, but remember, He respects your freedom to choose. It will grieve Him, but eventually He will back away.

That's why it's so important that you seek the Lord for every decision, not just a few major ones, but in every situation. You must always pray, "God, what is Your will in this? Show me and direct my steps." I promise you, when God directs your steps, it's not always going to be easy. You'll have to leave some things behind, stuff that is holding you back or people who would keep you from serving God, but it won't be long before you see how wise and wonderful your heavenly Father is.

When you choose to follow Jesus in every choice you make, you choose a life of integrity, moral purity, compassion toward others, and selflessness. You choose this life empowered by His Spirit to live a godly life, to be an effective witness, and to pray and believe God for miracles to heal the sick, cast out demons, and prophesy His love and encouragement into people's lives.

After all that serving, of course God will "add all these things unto you" (Matthew 6:33)! It is His joy and pleasure to provide everything you need and desire. There's no doubt about it: Choosing to make Jesus Christ your Lord and Savior is the most important choice of all, and walking with Him is how God's blessings flow bountifully into your life.

Receiving "All These Things"

From whence come wars and fightings among you? come they not hence, even of your lusts that war in your members?

Ye lust, and have not: ye kill, and desire to have, and cannot obtain: ye fight and war, yet ye have not, because ye ask not.

Ye ask, and receive not, because ye ask amiss, that ye may consume it upon your lusts.

James 4:1-3

Human beings will do the craziest things to get what they want or what they think they need. They'll even go to war with each other. There is a righteous reason to go to war, when God leads a nation to liberate another nation or defeat an enemy that is bent on destroying and conquering every nation in its path. But James is talking about going to war for unrighteous reasons, such as when nations lust after each other's land and resources.

Nations are not the only entities at war. People are often at war in their souls. This happens because they have never asked the Prince of Peace to take control of their lives. They don't know what it means to do the will of God and trust Him to add all they need to their lives.

Verse 2 says, "Ye fight and war, yet ye have not, because ye ask not." These people haven't turn to the One true God through Jesus Christ, to look to Him to supply all their needs. Verse 3 tells us that when they do ask, they don't receive because they ask for things according to their will and not God's will. All they can see is what they want, or "me, my, mine."

As the Lord was talking to me about this, I held up my hands and cried, "Guilty!" Don't we always pray for ourselves first? Maybe not always first, but certainly second! We pray for our needs and then, maybe, we pray for other people's needs. I can remember teaching people in prayer meetings, "Let's take the first five or ten minutes to get all the praying for our personal needs out of the way. Then we can concentrate on praying for our church, community, and nation."

As I reflected on this, the Lord took me right back to Matthew, chapter 6:

> Therefore take no thought, saying, What shall we eat? or, What shall we drink? or, Wherewithal shall we be clothed?
>
> (For after all these things do the Gentiles seek:) for your heavenly Father knoweth that ye have need of all these things.
>
> But seek ye first the kingdom of God, and his righteousness; and all these things shall be added unto you.
>
> Matthew 6:31-33

God said to me, "Your Father knows what you need before you ask."

I responded, "Then what do I need to ask for?"

He said, "Look at Job."

Job went through hell on earth, losing his children, his possessions, and his health. His wife was not much help. She told him to curse God and die! His friends tried to help, but they just made him feel worse. But at the end of the book, everything changed when Job saw the light. He took his eyes off of himself and all his problems and chose to pray for his friends.

> And the Lord turned the captivity of Job, when he prayed for his friends: also the Lord gave Job twice as much as he had before.
>
> Job 42:10

God didn't heal Job and restore all he'd lost when Job prayed for Job, or even when Job said to his friends, "Pray for me.

Everybody pray for me!" God moved on Job's behalf when he prayed for his friends.

We think we need something for ourselves or we need something to happen, but only God knows what we really need. We should, "Bear ye one another's burdens, and so fulfil the law of Christ" (Galatians 6:2). We need to turn our attention to our brothers and sisters and love and pray for one another. God wants us to start really caring for our friends in the Lord. That's seeking His kingdom and doing the right thing. It's the way His kingdom operates. His blessings flow into our lives when we allow His blessings to flow out of our lives to others.

Sometimes in order to love somebody, you've got to get God's perspective. Along with that, you have to shut your mouth until what comes out is pleasing to Him and in agreement with how He loves and cares for that person. The kingdom is about the King and His righteousness; it's not about you!

Instead of being critical in your heart and letting that poison your spirit, you need to go back to 1 Peter 3:10 and remember that you are to love life, the God-kind of life, by choosing to speak no evil. A critical, cynical spirit will kill your love for God and for people, so choose to get it out of your life. Then God can shower His blessings on you.

The Blessing of Life

For months, I had a condition in my eyes that caused my vision to get more and more blurry, even with glasses. My eyes were extremely dry, and I used all kinds of drops to keep them moist, but it seemed like nothing was helping.

Finally, I gave the problem to the Lord. I prayed, "God, this is Your temple and You're going to have to take care of it." A couple of days later, I stood in front of our congregation and said, "Whoa! I'm seeing! How many of you heard me say that I couldn't see past the first three rows? Well, I see you back there on the back row! I see every one of your faces this morning! Hallelujah!"

What happened? Resurrection life! The same Spirit who raised Jesus from the dead dwells in me and makes alive every cell in my body (Romans 8:11). His resurrection life healed my eyes. Because I chose to love the eternal life of God inside me and speak the truth and not evil, God's resurrection life healed my eyes and blessed me with sight.

You must choose to love the life God has given you!

When you choose to love life and speak life, God blesses you. He will hear you and deliver you. Hebrews 4:12 says that God's Word is alive and powerful. Praying and speaking God's Word releases His almighty, delivering power. The Word of God is like a double-edged sword. When you speak God's Word, you take the head off your enemies while bringing God's power to bear in your situation. That's how His double-edged sword works! His everlasting love and life overcomes anything the enemy throws at you.

Love the life of God inside you. Love people, God's people and the unbelievers who need the Lord. Speak no evil, including in your prayers. Pray according to the Word as the Spirit leads you. Make these right choices, and then your biggest problem will be what to do with all the blessings God is sending your way!

7

Our Wonderful Shepherd

I first went out in ministry with a team as their worship leader, but it didn't work out. They left me in Fort Worth and went to California without telling me. That's why it didn't work out! I had quit my job in Corpus Christi to go travel as part of their ministry, now there I was, alone in a strange city and without a job.

I wasn't old enough or wise enough to look at what I couldn't understand and say in faith, "Thank You, Jesus!" All I prayed was, "Oh my God, what am I going to do?" I didn't know that since I had committed all my ways to Him, God would lead me in a path of right choices. I didn't understand that He was separating me from that group to lead me into my true calling.

The pastor of the church where we had just ministered asked me to preach for him. I preached for a week, even though I had never preached for anyone for a full week. Then the pastor asked

71

me to stay another week! I thought, *Of course I'll stay. I don't have anywhere else to go!* We had revival in that little storefront church in Fort Worth, Texas. We experienced the outpouring of the Holy Spirit in a wonderful way, and I'll never forget it.

During the first few days, I would walk down the road to the convenience store and buy a couple of my favorite kind of candy bars as a reward. While walking back to the church one particular afternoon with one candy bar in my pocket and eating the other one, I prayed, "What am I going to do? Where am I going to go? I've left home. I made a big deal about it. I quit my job to go into the ministry."

Just then I heard the voice of the Holy Spirit say, "If you will trust Me, you will never need a man." By "man," I knew He meant a human. He went on, "You'll never need a man to put food in your mouth, clothes on your back, or shoes on your feet. I'll take care of you." I was encountering Jesus as my wonderful Shepherd.

I didn't yet understand that by choosing to trust Jesus to meet all my needs in every situation, obeying Him in what He'd called me to do, I was seeking first His kingdom and His righteousness. That meant that "all these things," everything I would ever need in life, would be given to me.

Later, I was on my way to Chicago to preach, and I drove into a terrible snowstorm. Being from south Texas, I had only seen snow once, briefly in Houston. I certainly had never driven in it. I was by myself, except for my little poodle that traveled with me. As soon as I saw a roadside motel, I stopped. The motel consisted of a little circle of cabins that were really like shacks.

I went into the office to get a room for the night, and a creaky old man opened the creaky old door to one of those creaky old shacks. I remember the long, old key he gave me. As soon as he left, I locked the door, moved the dresser in front of the door, got in bed with my dog, and pulled the covers up over us!

This was my prayer: "Dear God, there's not a soul in this world who knows where I am tonight or even cares. Nobody! Nobody but You, Lord. You're the only one who knows where I am." Again, I encountered my wonderful Shepherd. Today, He still knows right where I am and makes sure I have everything I need.

I've told you these stories to illustrate something. As long as you are following the Lord with your whole heart, making right choices, He will be with you and take care of you. That is something you really need to know and cling to as the world we live in gets crazier and crazier. You have a wonderful, wonderful Shepherd!

No Condemnation

There is therefore now no condemnation to them which are in Christ Jesus, who walk not after the flesh, but after the Spirit.

Romans 8:1

We have talked about the fact that when your conscience is clear and you are making right choices, you can boldly go into the throne room of God and pray. You can talk to the Lord with no baggage holding you down. No blame, judgment, or sin is keeping you from speaking freely and openly with Him.

Of course, if you have made some wrong choices, all you need to do is repent, turn away from your sin, and come back into the Lord's presence and favor. He will never turn you away! But He will always say what He said throughout the Gospels: "Go, and sin no more." He will tell you the truth; you may be righteous through His blood, but you must act righteous if you want to live free of condemnation, guilt, and shame.

Listening to and obeying the Holy Spirit is a wonderful way to live. You are free inside and feel clean, clear, and open to all possibilities. That's so much better than constantly saying to yourself, "I haven't read my Bible in a week. I haven't prayed in a month. I watched that horrible movie, and now I can't get it out of my mind. I told my sister she looked like a pig and never took the trash out like my dad told me. I told my boss I didn't feel well, but I was really late because I was hung over." The list of sins goes on and on!

If you want to get out from under all that garbage, you need to start by choosing to repent, and then continue to make right choices from moment to moment. You won't believe how good you will feel when you are living right and sense God's pleasure!

For to be carnally minded is death; but to be spiritually minded is life and peace.

Romans 8:6

Being carnally minded will kill your hopes, your dreams, your faith in God, and even your life. I'd say that the alternative is a much better choice! Be spiritually minded, and then you will walk in life—the God kind of life—and in peace that goes beyond your understanding.

Everyone's Psalm?

There's one psalm that even atheists request to be read at their funeral. I guess they think of it as "good literature," which it is; but if you've never acknowledged, known, loved, or served the

Shepherd, you will never truly understand the 23rd Psalm. Unbelievers don't realize that this powerful passage of "good literature" doesn't apply to them. The psalm is comprised of just six verses, but it beautifully describes our wonderful relationship with Jesus as we follow Him in making right choices.

The LORD is my shepherd; I shall not want.

He maketh me to lie down in green pastures: he leadeth me beside the still waters.

He restoreth my soul: he leadeth me in the paths of righteousness for his name's sake.

Yea, though I walk through the valley of the shadow of death, I will fear no evil: for thou art with me; thy rod and thy staff they comfort me.

Thou preparest a table before me in the presence of mine enemies: thou anointest my head with oil; my cup runneth over.

Surely goodness and mercy shall follow me all the days of my life: and I will dwell in the house of the LORD for ever.

Let's consider these key phrases indepth.

The Lord is my shepherd.

When the Lord is your shepherd, you go where He goes and do what He does. You say what He prompts you to say. You don't do your own thing, say whatever comes to your mind, and let your mind wander into all kinds of evil images and ideas. You stick with your Shepherd. This verse speaks first of righteousness. As His righteous sheep, you make right choices.

I shall not want.

A shepherd is a herdsman. He guides the sheep and cares for them. He sees that they are well fed and watered, that they are safe and secure. If a sheep goes off on its own, it can starve, get hurt, and die. A smart sheep stays with its shepherd! It knows that only with the shepherd can it want for nothing. Everything it needs, all the pleasures of life, belong to that sheep as long as it stays with the shepherd.

He maketh me to lie down in green pastures.

Green is the color that speaks of life, growth, and health. The Good Shepherd's green pastures are filled with great food. We can munch all day and night on His Word and rest in peace. Our Shepherd wants us to rest inside and out. He doesn't want us running around in a panic, worrying about every little thing. He says, "Come unto me, all ye that labour and are heavy laden, and I will give you rest" (Matthew 11:28). He wants to take all our heavy burdens on His shoulders. He wants us to rest in Him no matter what we're going through, because He has got it all under control.

He leadeth me beside the still waters.

Still waters are calm and soothing. They quench every thirst and make us content and satisfied. This mention of water also refers to the Word of God. In Ephesians 5, Paul likens a husband and wife to Jesus and His Church, and writes:

> **That he might sanctify and cleanse it [the Church] with the washing of water by the word,**

That he might present it to himself a glorious church, not having spot, or wrinkle, or any such thing; but that it should be holy and without blemish.

Ephesians 5:26-27 [explanation mine]

Jesus leads us to drink of His Word so we will grow up in Him and make decisions in line with what the Scriptures say. Second Peter 1:4 says that reading, studying, and believing God's Word is the same as partaking of His divine nature. Our Bridegroom wants us to be righteous inside and out, holy and without blemish. That's why He leads us to the still waters of His Word.

He restoreth my soul.

Jesus is transforming us daily by His Holy Spirit.

But the Comforter, which is the Holy Ghost, whom the Father will send in my name, he shall teach you all things, and bring all things to your remembrance, whatsoever I have said unto you.

Peace I leave with you, my peace I give unto you: not as the world giveth, give I unto you. Let not your heart be troubled, neither let it be afraid.

John 14:26-27

What a great gift the Holy Spirit is! He teaches us how to think, speak, and act just like Jesus. Under His control, our emotions stay steady, and we can think clearly to do the right thing and continue to rest in Him. Any problem we have can be solved and our souls restored to peace and tranquility.

He leadeth me in the paths of righteousness for his name's sake.

Our Shepherd only gives us one path to take—the right path. He leads us to make right choices, to manifest His righteousness as we walk through life. There are many paths that are illegal, immoral, and selfish; but the Lord's path is right and good. That's the path He is pointing us to, and He does it for His name's sake; for the sake of Jehovah, the God who saves. He doesn't kill, steal, and destroy. He gives life, abundant life. He gives us the grace to make right choices, so He gets all the glory!

Yea, though I walk through the valley of the shadow of death, I will fear no evil: for thou art with me.

The key word here is *through*. If I shot at a wall and there was a bullet hole on my side of the wall but no bullet hole on the other side of the wall, we would know that the bullet was somewhere in that wall. It didn't go through. It got stuck. David wrote, "Though I walk *through*," because he knew God would take him all the way through the valley to glory. He knew he had nothing to fear because his Shepherd was with him. "I will fear no evil, for thou art with me" is the confession of a right-choice man!

Thy rod and thy staff they comfort me.

The rod is used to tap the sheep to keep them going in the right direction. The staff has a crook in it, so if a sheep starts to go in the wrong direction, the shepherd can use the staff to take hold of the neck of that sheep and pull it back into line. If the sheep manages to run away and falls in a hole, the crook can be used to lift the sheep out and bring it back to safety. Our Shepherd's rod is the Holy Spirit, who leads us and guides us. His staff is His Word, which delivers us from the snares and deceptions of the enemy. Thank God for His rod and staff! Nothing comforts me more than to know He is always with me, to keep me on the paths of righteousness by His Spirit and His Word.

Thou preparest a table before me in the presence of mine enemies.

What God has for you is always in front of you. Your meal, everything you need to defeat the enemy, is not in your past. Live for Him right now. Make the right choice for this moment. You don't have anything to fear, because whenever you encounter temptation or feel your life slipping away, your Shepherd will have a table full of everything you need to resist the devil and flee, to be healed and set free.

Too many Christians are walking around in a quagmire of thoughts of all the things that could go wrong in the world in the days to come. That's not proper thinking; that's just plain old fear! God isnow won't face We need to make the right choice and have complete faith in God's Word. He will have that table all set for us when the time comes, and we will get through it!

Thou anointest my head with oil.

In the Bible, oil is a type of the Holy Spirit. We all want to be anointed by the Holy Spirit, especially if we're facing a trial or temptation. But this scripture means more than that.

During worship one morning, I was impressed to ask the sister next to me, "Sister Mary, when the shepherd poured oil on the head of the sheep, what was it for?"

She answered, "Well, that oil helped keep all the bugs and gnats out of the sheep's wool." Are you "bugged" by something? Have you laid down with dogs and gotten up with fleas? Then you need to ask the Holy Spirit to flow over your mind and heart and drive out the bugs!

Sister Mary went on to say, "The shepherd pours that oil on the sheep and it's soothing, but also healing." What does the Word tell us to do when someone is sick?

Is any sick among you? let him call for the elders of the church; and let them pray over him, anointing him with oil in the name of the Lord:

And the prayer of faith shall save the sick, and the Lord shall raise him up; and if he have committed sins, they shall be forgiven him.

James 5:14-15

If you are sick or need to confess some sin so that it can't bother you anymore, call for the elders to anoint you with oil in the name of the Lord. All those gnats and bugs will fly off of you, and you will be healthy, happy, and free to serve the Lord with gladness.

My cup runneth over.

God is more than enough! He gives life that is abundant and beyond what we can ask, think, or even imagine. The joy, peace, contentment, satisfaction, and overwhelming love of the Lord is indescribable. Truly, this is the greatest motivation to always seek God's righteousness by making right choices.

Surely goodness and mercy shall follow me all the days of my life.

What have we been seeing about making right choices and following the Lord on the path of righteousness? God's goodness and His mercy will follow us always! Even when we fall into a ditch, He will be there to get us out with His rod and staff. He will set us back on our feet and get us going in the right direction again. We are loved! We are forgiven! We are the apple of His eye!

And I will dwell in the house of the Lord for ever.

This is the bottom line: Where will you go when you die? Thank God I received the Lord in that tent meeting years ago! Yes, sometimes it is all I can do to follow my Shepherd and submit to His rod and staff, but I know where I'm going when all is said and done. I know He's preparing a place for me in Heaven and all the struggles and difficulties and terrors I face in this world will be gone forever. Praise the Lord! I love my wonderful, wonderful Shepherd!

8

Sowing and Reaping

It is wonderful to live for God with no condemnation. As you let the Holy Spirit direct your steps, allowing God's Word to renew your mind and restore your soul, you know you are pleasing to God. He is making a way before you and will fight your battles because you are making right choices. Nothing pleases Him more than to see His righteousness coming forth in your attitudes, your talk, and everything you do. When He sees this, He can do His favorite thing—bless you!

In Genesis, God gives us a law that rules His creation:

> **While the earth remaineth, seedtime and harvest, and cold and heat, and summer and winter, and day and night shall not cease.**

> **Genesis 8:22**

As long as the earth is still here, the seasons will continue. The sun will shine during the day, the moon will shine at night, and the law of seedtime and harvest will still be in effect.

Be not deceived; God is not mocked: for whatsoever a man soweth, that shall he also reap.

For he that soweth to his flesh shall of the flesh reap corruption; but he that soweth to the Spirit shall of the Spirit reap life everlasting.

And let us not be weary in well doing: for in due season we shall reap, if we faint not.

As we have therefore opportunity, let us do good unto all men, especially unto them who are of the household of faith.

Galatians 6:7-10

The minute you mention sowing and reaping, many believers start to groan and think you're talking about money. "Oh no! Now the preacher is going to put a guilt trip on me if I don't give, or she's going to tell me I'll get whatever I want if I just donate every week to her ministry." First of all, that's a bad attitude that God cannot bless. Read Galatians 6:7-10 again. It's not talking about money; it's talking about relationships. "Do good unto all men, especially unto them who are of the household of faith" (verse 10). Nothing pleases the Lord more than when we treat each other well.

I have learned many valuable things about how to live my life for Jesus by reading the stories of people who have had near death experiences. These accounts stir you up to remember that your time on earth is short and precious, so you don't want to waste a second of it. In his book *Imagine Heaven*, John Burke gives a biblical picture of Heaven and alongside that, recounts different people's near-death experiences. One thing really struck me. Most of the people Burke interviewed said that as they were dying, their whole life flashed before them just like a movie on a screen, but what surprised them was seeing what God thought was important. They didn't see all their successes, the times they won awards, got big promotions, or built a great career. They saw how they'd treated the people in their lives. What was most important to God was what they'd sown into and reaped from other people's lives.

God doesn't care if you make a lot of money, rise to great power in the government, or become a celebrity everyone thinks is the best-looking person on earth. That's fine with Him, but that's not His great concern. He also doesn't care if you live a quiet life without great fortune, fame, or influence. He just wants you to fulfill the destiny He created you to fulfill and express His love and goodness to everyone you meet along the way, especially to those of "the household of faith."

The Household of Faith

Sometimes we forget that our real and eternal family is not our natural family, but is the body of Christ. We pray our natural family all gets born again, but our real and eternal family is comprised of our brothers and sisters in the Lord. We aren't a household that runs on strife, jealousy, and competition; we are a household that trusts God for ourselves and each other. We are a household of faith.

In Matthew 6:33, Jesus said to seek first the kingdom of God and His righteousness. There's no kingdom without a king, but there's also no kingdom without people! A king can sit around all day and proclaim he's king, but if no one is following him and his land has no people living in it, his kingdom doesn't really exist. A real kingdom is made up of real people.

If you're going to seek first God's kingdom, that means you're going to consider His people who make up His kingdom. With that in mind, you can understand that seeking His righteousness isn't just about making right choices for you; it's also about making right choices where other people are concerned, especially your brothers and sisters in the Lord. They have been washed in the blood of the Lamb, just like you. Jesus died for them, too. You should have the same love and respect for them that He does.

> Finally, be ye all of one mind, having compassion one of another, love as brethren, be pitiful, be courteous:
>
> Not rendering evil for evil, or railing for railing: but contrariwise blessing; knowing that ye are thereunto called, that ye should inherit a blessing.
>
> 1 Peter 3:8-9

I have never been so stirred in my heart as I have been over this message of righteousness. God has been talking to me especially about how we treat one another, about making right choices in our relationships. In His kingdom, seeking His righteousness, we can't all be of one mind unless we have compassion for each other. In His kingdom, we must follow our King and love one another unconditionally the way He loves us. Since Jesus loved us so much that He died for us, that's a tall order!

There are some brothers and sisters I would die for in a heartbeat. I would take a bullet for them without hesitation. I love them. They are a tremendous blessing to me. And then there are others.... Let's just say there are some people in the body of Christ who give me much less of a thrill. Some just aren't "my kind of people." They love the Lord, but they do it differently than I do. Some rub me the wrong way. Others I wouldn't trust to walk my dog because I see them continually making wrong choices. They say they're trying and always ask for prayer, but they never seem to get their lives in order.

This is my challenge! I don't know where I originally read this, but I put this quote on my Facebook page: "When you're getting ready to put somebody down, put them down on your prayer list first." If I'm having trouble loving or respecting someone, I've learned to start praying for them.

When I sow prayer into someone's life, I reap love and goodness. It isn't long before I begin to love them as God does and can see what He put in them, their gifts and callings, their dreams and desires. I see their divine potential and begin to have faith that God can do something great with them.

I can tell you that there are some people only God can help. They aren't going to listen to you, but they might hear God's voice through someone He sends. Sowing prayer is the same as sowing love and all God's blessings into someone's life. When I find myself being critical of a brother or a sister or the person who is holding up the checkout line when I'm in a hurry, I have learned to bite my tongue and turn that thought pattern off in my head. I make the right choice to not think or speak anything bad about people.

My nephew came to live with me when he was eleven. One Sunday afternoon he asked me *in that tone*, "Do I have to go to church tonight?" That rubbed me the wrong way, and I turned around to let him have it. I was about to say, "Listen buddy, I'll pack your bag and send you back to your mother tomorrow!"

Just as I turned, the Holy Spirit said, "Don't you ever threaten to send him home. He is home." Well, that closed my mouth, and I learned a valuable lesson. Too often we get on our high horse and do more harm than good in the name of the Lord. Yes, I believe in going to church. It's a necessary part of our spiritual growth, but that young boy needed love, not offense, to show him the way.

Thank God I obeyed the Holy Spirit. Today, my nephew is a pastor! I'm so glad I sowed into His life from the Spirit and not from my flesh. The joy of seeing him serving God is what I am reaping today.

First Peter 3:8 says we are to be "pitiful" to one another, but that doesn't mean what we think it means. We are to be tender-hearted, understanding, and give one another the benefit of the doubt. There might be something going on in a person's life that we don't know about. Even if people treat us badly, we should forgive them, bring them to God in prayer, and be friendly and kind. There have been times when I have been stunned at what another person has gone through or is going through.

There was a minister I had known for almost twenty years, who never impressed me much. I never thought much about her life or ministry. One day I heard her giving her personal testimony to a person sitting right beside me, and I sat there with my mouth open and tears in my eyes. I had no idea what she had been through. I thought, *Why didn't I know this?* And then I remembered. At the time she was going through her trial, I had been going through a trial myself. I didn't see anybody else's hurt, because I was caught up in my own ordeal.

After that, I had such a love for that person. Today, we text each other, we talk, and we have a wonderful relationship in the Lord. This humbled me! How many people had I passed over because I did not take the time to ask them what they were going through or because I could not know what was happening in their lives? How many had I ignored because I was too involved in my own life to consider theirs?

All you can do when you come to this point is fall on the altar, repent, and allow the Holy Spirit to rule your heart and mind even more than He did before. We cannot sow rightly into the lives of others unless we follow the Spirit. He may not want us to befriend someone; He may want us to stay away and just pray for them. In order to make the right choices in our relationships, only the Holy Spirit can tell us what to say and what to do. Sometimes we think we know what is best for someone, but only He knows what is best for each one of us.

The Simple "Stop" Sign

Let's look at 1 Peter 3:8-9 again:

Finally, be ye all of one mind, having compassion one of another, love as brethren, be pitiful, be courteous:

Not rendering evil for evil, or railing for railing: but contrariwise blessing; knowing that ye are thereunto called, that ye should inherit a blessing.

There is one word that will stop us from rendering evil for evil and railing for railing: courtesy. If we start every day with the intention of just being courteous to everyone we meet, showing them respect and having good manners, we will be able to stop ourselves from getting mixed up in conversations and situations that are far from right choices.

If someone spreads a rumor about you that isn't true, don't start spreading a rumor about them. Instead, forgive them, pray for them, and then do something nice for them. The Holy Spirit might have you go to them and say, "I heard you were telling people this about me, and I know you would never want to hurt me, so I thought I'd come to you right away so you could know the truth." Bless that person. Treat them like a friend, like you would want to be treated. Don't return evil for evil.

When people are talking about politics or religion, a conversation can get heated real fast. When someone with an opposite view from yours begins railing on you for your beliefs or opinion, the temptation is to jump in and rail right back. Blow both barrels of truth right through them! But that's not the way we win people to the Lord or encourage our brothers and sisters.

You know what *railing* means? It means *bitter* complaint or violent denunciation. It's assaulting someone with words. If someone is railing on you, just smile and let them wonder what in the world you're thinking about. They know that their yelling shouldn't make anybody smile. Your smile can act like a mirror to help them see that they are just being ugly.

But you must be aware that sometimes a smile can be construed as taunting them or laughing at what they are saying. This will only make them angrier. Listen for the guidance of the Holy Spirit. There are times the Holy Spirit will have you listen quietly to let the person know you respect their opinion. Some people scream because they feel like no one ever listens to them. You could be the first person they've come across who listens and respects their opinion, which gives you a lot of influence for the Lord in their life.

If we want others to make right choices toward us and treat us courteously, then we must be courteous. That means sowing a good choice into their lives and not returning their railing. We need to stay calm, show respect for their ideas, and leave the rest to God. My experience is that no one can turn hearts and minds the way He can!

First Peter 3:8-9 says that when we sow pity (understanding and compassion) and courtesy (kindness and good manners) into other people's lives, especially when this has not been done to us, we will inherit a blessing. We will reap blessing when we sow blessing. Blessing may or may not come through the people to whom we showed God's love, but we know God will bless us when we choose to do the right thing.

I know showing goodness, mercy, and respect when you're under attack is not easy to do! In fact, it's impossible. You can't do it in your own strength. That's why you need to seek God's kingdom and His righteousness. You need His miracle-working power to bless instead of curse when the whole world is putting you down.

I can tell you from experience that the Holy Spirit will always inspire you and empower you to make the right choice in a terrible situation. In emotional times when it seems like Jesus is your only friend, the Holy Spirit will gently ask you to consider what the other person or persons are going through and be courteous to them. If you don't know what they are going through, He may tell you; or, He may give you His compassion for them.

If you have any doubts about what you are sowing into someone's life, just look at Jesus. He sowed His very life for your eternal life. He gave Himself so He could reap a harvest of souls for His Father's kingdom. His commitment and selflessness should mark all the choices we make toward others, and when they do, there is no imagining what we will reap in our lifetime and for eternity.

9

Living by Faith

Wherefore the law was our schoolmaster to bring us unto Christ, that we might be justified by faith.

But after that faith is come, we are no longer under a schoolmaster.

For ye are all the children of God by faith in Christ Jesus.

For as many of you as have been baptized into Christ have put on Christ.

Galatians 3:24-27

There comes a time when we become mature, when we no longer need to be reminded that it is a sin to murder or steal. We take responsibility for ourselves and the choices we make. The Law showed us that we were sinners, and then by grace through faith we were born again (Ephesians 2:8). After that, we should show the world that we have "put on Christ."

Jesus lived by faith. He made choices in line with His faith in God the Father and all His promises. Now our part is to make right choices through our faith in God and His Word. Seeking the kingdom and His righteousness is living by faith.

Living by faith can only happen if your spirit and soul get the right food. You need to eat God's Word and drink in His Spirit, because whatever you put into your mind and heart is what you will become. If you are habitually giving in to your flesh and eating and drinking what the world and the devil put in front of you, you are being conformed to the world. Don't fall for the lie that you can live any way you want and still build your life upon the rock. Jesus put the foundation under you when you were saved, but you have to stay on it to build something that's truly good and lasting. Too many of us wander away and then wonder why the ground is shifting underneath our feet. We heard the Word, but didn't live it.

> Therefore whosoever heareth these sayings of mine, and doeth them, I will liken him unto a wise man, which built his house upon a rock:
>
> And the rain descended, and the floods came, and the winds blew, and beat upon that house; and it fell not: for it was founded upon a rock.
>
> And every one that heareth these sayings of mine, and doeth them not, shall be likened unto a foolish man, which built his house upon the sand:
>
> And the rain descended, and the floods came, and the winds blew, and beat upon that house; and it fell: and great was the fall of it.
>
> Matthew 7:24-27

For your life to be built upon the rock, you need to abide in the Rock of your salvation, the Living Word. You need to spend some quality time every day praying in the Spirit, and then pray whenever the unction comes. Your focus must stay on the Lord, so you can do His will and not get off track. His Word is the rock of revelation upon which you will stand and overcome. Being born again puts you on the rock, but seeking first His kingdom and His righteousness, making right choices, is what grows you and secures you on the rock.

I'm not saying you will lose your salvation if you don't read your Bible and pray every day. Your salvation didn't come by your works, so you can't lose it by your works. However, your life in Christ will be a sad sight to see if you just get born again and then live like the world. You probably won't fulfill your calling because you will never know who you really are in Christ. You will also probably be miserable and dissatisfied. What's worse, when you stand before God on the Judgment Day, you'll have no rewards and a bonfire of wood, hay, and stubble.

> For other foundation can no man lay than that is laid, which is Jesus Christ.
>
> Now if any man build upon this foundation gold, silver, precious stones, wood, hay, stubble;
>
> every man's work shall be made manifest: for the day shall declare it, because it shall be revealed by fire; and the fire shall try every man's work of what sort it is.
>
> If any man's work abide which he hath built thereupon, he shall receive a reward.

If any man's work shall be burned, he shall suffer loss: but he himself shall be saved; yet so as by fire.

1 Corinthians 3:11-15

On the Day of Judgment, all your works will be tried by fire. The things you did for God, living by faith in Him, will be gold, silver, and precious stones. They will not burn. The wrong choices that you made, all the things you did trusting yourself or someone else, will be wood, hay, and stubble. They will burn up in God's righteous fire, because works not of faith in God are not righteous. They are not His will and Romans 14:23 says that whatever is not of faith is sin.

Don't build a bonfire out of your life! You don't want to just be "saved, yet so as by fire." You don't want to smell like smoke, with ashes falling off of you. Stay in God's Word and pray without ceasing because you love Jesus. g Do it because Jesus saved you from eternal damnation and loves you more than anyone ever has or will love you. Do it because you want to live up to the potential He has put inside you.

When I was first born again, I immediately loved God's Word and would read it every time I had the chance. I kept a little New Testament in my desk drawer and during my lunch hour, I would read the Bible while I ate my sandwich and apple. The company told me they didn't want me to read my Bible at my desk, because I was the receptionist and the first person anyone coming in would see. I obeyed, but I continued to devour my Bible whenever I could.

I learned about who I was as a child of God, how to walk with God and talk with Him, and how to live my life in the world. That was when I learned that I shouldn't marry an unbeliever and all the other boundaries of love God set around me. I knew that in order to please Him and have a good life, I had to obey His Word. Today I understand that abiding in God's Word is the same as abiding in Jesus. I love the Word because I love Jesus.

We know from Romans 10:17 that faith comes by hearing the Word of God, but what does loving Jesus have to do with faith? Galatians 5:6 says that faith works by love. Have you ever noticed that when you are angry with someone or sad about something and start to read the Bible, your mood begins to change? The jealousy, frustration, and fear melt away as God's unconditional *agape* love takes hold of your heart.

Faith in God rises up because faith works by love! Suddenly, you marvel at how you could have been so bent out of shape when God loves you so much. Your faith in Him soars when His love abounds, and right choices become clearer and so much easier to make.

No More Shame

Living by faith does not mean we don't need to read the Word of God anymore; it means we need God's Word more than ever. Today, I need the wisdom of my Bible to be certain I am truly seeking God's kingdom and His righteousness and haven't gone off on some rabbit trail.

When Paul was just about to be executed, he asked Timothy to bring him the scrolls of the Word of God so he could study them (2 Timothy 4:13). He was abiding in God's Word when he took his last breath on earth and his first breath in Heaven. That's the way we all need to be!

We need to study the Word as well as read it. For those of us in full-time ministry, it is our job to study. We have to immerse ourselves in the Word so that we can teach it and break it down for our congregations and the people to whom we minister. But we still have to live it just like everyone else.

If you make your living as a car mechanic or doctor or school teacher, it might be harder to make time to study the Word, but there are lots of applications and study helps for your smart phone and tablets today that people didn't have when I got saved. All we had were big books to read—commentaries, concordances, and lexicons. Today all these materials are easy to access from anywhere.

Study to shew thyself approved unto God, a workman that needeth not to be ashamed, rightly dividing the word of truth.

2 Timothy 2:15

These words from 2 Timothy are some of the last Paul wrote before he died. Paul told Timothy that studying the Word of God would keep him from being ashamed because he would make right choices in agreement with God's thoughts and ways. Studying God's Word would keep him focused on pleasing God rather than himself, make him productive in everything he did, and keep him happy and content. When you don't know God's Word, you can't answer the questions of unbelievers. Often, people who don't know God are curious about what it means to be born again and what the born-again, Bible-thumping crowd believes. If you don't study your Bible and continually grow in the understanding of God's Word, you will not be able to give unbelievers a satisfactory answer to their questions. You may even become ashamed of the Gospel. That is sad! If you really love Jesus and you really love people, you are going to want to bring them together! You are going to make the right choices to live in God's Word, pray in the Spirit, and take advantage of every opportunity God gives you to share the Good News of Jesus.

It takes faith—sometimes great faith—to make the right choice and tell someone the truth about their eternal life. Sometimes you have to come right out and say, "If you don't receive Jesus as your Lord and Savior, you're going to be separated from God forever when you die and go to hell." You must have faith in God to speak His truth in love!

How do you get that kind of faith? Study God's Word. Then, the Holy Spirit can open the doors and give you the right words to say that will touch the hearts of people and bring them to Jesus. Living by faith changes lives!

Faith and Obedience

After walking with the Lord for a while, we come to know He is faithful to keep His promises. We have confidence in doing His will and making the right choice. Living by faith means growing up in obedience, learning to get past all the fears and other hindrances. Every time you crucify your flesh to make the right choice, you are exercising your faith in God. Over time, your faith gets stronger and stronger. Obeying the Lord is the spiritual equivalent of working out at the gym. Every act of obedience done in faith, stretches and builds up your faith.

Sometimes we learn the hard way. We think we can disobey and get away with it, and then God has to discipline us. After you've been disciplined by the Lord, you never want to disobey Him again!

And ye have forgotten the exhortation which speaketh unto you as unto children, My son, despise not thou the chastening of the Lord, nor faint when thou art rebuked of him:

For whom the Lord loveth he chasteneth, and scourgeth every son whom he receiveth.

Furthermore we have had fathers of our flesh which corrected us, and we gave them reverence: shall we not much rather be in subjection unto the Father of spirits, and live?

Hebrews 12:5-6, 9

When I was a little girl, I played with the kids in my neighborhood. Back then, you could roam around and play with the neighbor kids, and it was safe. My mother's law was that when it started to get dark, I had to come home. One day I was playing down the street and around the corner from our house. We were having a great time, and I didn't notice when it was getting dark. All of a sudden, I looked up and saw an adult coming toward us. She wasn't close enough for my friends to recognize who it was, but I knew! I knew my mother's walk.

Just before she got to me, she turned aside to a little bush, broke off a small branch, and cleaned it of all the twigs and leaves. Then she took me by my hand and switched my legs all the way home. But that wasn't the end of it! When we got in the house, she took me in the bathroom and washed my mouth out with soap. She said, "You will never again forget that I told you to come home when it is dark." And I never did!

After my mother disciplined me, I made the right choice to get home before dark. As I grew older and made more and more right choices, my mother gave me more freedom. By the time I was a teenager, she let me set my curfews. I had earned her trust and grown strong in character. How did this happen? First, I truly knew my mother loved me. Second, I respected the fact that she was older and wiser than I was. Faith works by love and honor, so I obeyed her.

When my mother disciplined me, was she being mean to me? Absolutely not! She loved me enough to deter me from placing myself in a compromised situation. I'm grateful to have had an earthly mother who showed me the purpose of discipline.

Our Father is the same way. Because He loves us and doesn't want us to be harmed, He will discipline us when we disobey Him and put ourselves in harm's way. He doesn't discipline us with sickness or accidents. We cause those ourselves by walking away from Him. God disciplines us with His Word. One verse can pierce your heart and cause you to repent immediately. He always speaks the truth in love, and oh, what a relief it is! He is the best Father. Now that my daughter and nephew are both grown, there would be something really wrong with them and with me if I still had to teach them some of the same lessons I've been teaching since they were young. They know the right thing to do. They have matured and developed integrity because of their faith and obedience.

It works the same way with a believer and our Heavenly Father. When we trust in His love and knowledge of all things, we can obey Him in faith. As we grow in our faith and become more and more like Jesus, when we seek first His kingdom and His righteousness, all things are added—including maturity.

From Schoolmaster to Lord

Wherefore the law was our schoolmaster to bring us unto Christ, that we might be justified by faith.

But after that faith is come, we are no longer under a schoolmaster.

For ye are all the children of God by faith in Christ Jesus.

For as many of you as have been baptized into Christ have put on Christ.

Galatians 3:24-27

God is good and His Law is good. He gave us His Law to be our schoolmaster, but when I became His child, everything changed. My spirit became alive to Him personally and His Spirit came to live inside me. Now I am no longer under the "dead letter" of the Law; I am under Him. In fact, Ephesians 1 says I am "in Him." That's altogether different from reading a law and trying to obey it.

In Him, I am aware of His love, His wisdom, and His desire to bless me and keep me safe. We communicate so that I know His will and what path He wants me to take. The Bible contains the Law, and when I read it, it is alive and powerful. God's Word fills me with faith and inspires me to obey Him in all things, making right choices that please Him. I am constantly amazed at His manifold wisdom!

As I mature, the Word of God rises up within me when difficult choices come, and I know the Spirit of God is bringing to remembrance just what I need for that occasion. Then it is up to me to make the right choice. You see, it is not enough to hear God; we must obey God. As James tells us, faith without works is dead (James 2:14, 20, 26).

This is why Jesus told us to seek first His kingdom and His righteousness. We find out what the Word and the Spirit are saying as we study and pray in the Spirit. This builds our faith. This is seeking His kingdom, His rule, His will. Then we obey. We make the right choice.

When Jesus is your Lord and you are living by faith, you will make right choices. You will not be ashamed of the Gospel; you will not be a rebellious, whiny, crying baby Christian. You will grow up, put away all wickedness, and have good answers for those who ask about your faith. Living by faith is making right choices!

10

Divine Clothes

I put on righteousness, and it clothed me: my judgment was as a robe and a diadem.

Job 29:14

I clearly saw from what the Word told me and from the consequences of my actions that seeking first God's kingdom and His righteousness brought all kinds of blessings into my life. Then I read Job 29:14 and saw even more: my right choices, or putting on righteousness, literally gave me spiritual clothes.

Isaiah said the same thing:

I will greatly rejoice in the Lord, my soul shall be joyful in my God; for he hath clothed me with the garments of salvation, he hath covered me with the robe of righteousness, as a bridegroom decketh himself with ornaments, and as a bride adorneth herself with her jewels.

Isaiah 61:10

The moment we were born again our whole being was clothed in a robe of righteousness made from heavenly material. Job 29:14 says these spiritual clothes include a diadem, which is a headdress. That means we are holy and righteous in the sight of God from the top of our heads to the tip of our toes. He has clothed us with His own holiness. Now that ought to make you shout!

This knowledge should also make us take heed to what and how we think, speak, and act. Job 29:14 says that our righteous clothes cover all our decisions, all the judgments we make throughout our day. The first thing on our minds in any situation should be the Lord's will. When we acknowledge His will first and foremost, we show that we have put on His robe of righteousness, our divine clothes.

Children of God are spiritually dressed like royalty, so we ought to act like royalty. We should not be thugs, bullies, bigots, and snobs. We should be like our King, who always makes the right decision. When we reflect His image, not only does this bring His power, pleasure, and blessing into our lives, but also it brings His protection. We are safe when we live like citizens of God's kingdom, clothed in righteousness.

Right choices will keep you warm when it is cold, just like a warm coat. Right choices will shield you from evil, like supernatural armor. The divine clothes you wear are activated when you make godly decisions, and all the power of Heaven moves to keep you safe and on the right path.

Divine Timing

There are times when God speaks or gives us a word of prophecy, and we know there is timing involved. We may need to go through a process before we actually step into what was prophesied for us to do. But there are other times when we need to practice instant obedience. This is how we demonstrate that we are clothed with righteousness.

One day I pulled up to a Hallmark store to buy a birthday card and noticed this precious old lady sitting outside. She was obviously homeless, sitting next to her rusty grocery cart that contained all her worldly possessions. Just then I heard the Holy Spirit say, "Give her $100.00."

I said, "Who me?"

He said, "She needs it more than you do."

I didn't give myself time to think about it or talk myself out of it. I just reached into my purse and pulled out a $100.00 bill. Then I got out of the car and walked over to the lady. As I handed the money to her I said, "God told me to give you this. He told me that you need it more than I do." The woman looked shocked. I think she wanted one of those markers to make sure the bill was real!

I went into the store and bought a card, and the woman was still sitting there when I came out. I waved at her, went on my way, and never saw her again.

This incident made me think about how many times the Lord wants us to bless others and reveal His love and goodness, but we hesitate or wait too long. Sometimes we are so caught up in our own lives that we don't hear the Lord's instruction. But often, we hear Him, faith comes, and we wait too long to obey. When we realize we missed it, our hearts regret it for days and we may even start to think perhaps we didn't hear from God after all.

Faith can die if you don't act on the word of the Lord or the instruction of the Holy Spirit right away. Most of the time, if you hear God and know it's God, faith comes at that moment to do whatever He is telling you to do. You have to act before fear, doubt, or natural thinking comes to steal the word and the faith to do God's will.

I believe there is a special blessing when you act on God's Word immediately in all the little things that happen during your day. Somebody will say, "Well, I want a confirmation." These people get four confirmations and three prophecies and still don't obey!

Often obedience is painful to the flesh, like giving $100.00 to a stranger or stopping to pray for a friend when you have so many "important" things to do. However, the joys of instant obedience are great and everlasting. Only when you get to Heaven will you know all the rewards and blessings that came because of your simple act of obedience. Remember what happens when you throw a very small pebble into a pond!

"But what if what I heard was a demon or just my own idea and not God's?" If a demon is behind what you've heard, the Holy Spirit will give you a check in your spirit. If it's your own thought and that thought is in line with God's Word and you have no check in your spirit, go with it! Even if you miss it, God knows your heart is in the right place. He will work it all for your good because you love Him and are seeking first His righteousness. You've got the right clothes on!

God or Mammon?

You don't want your divine clothes to get dirty. We had a man in our congregation once who came into the church when he was really struggling financially. He was a businessman who had lost everything and was starting over. Bishop John prayed with the man, and he got a job where he began to prosper.

The man got back on his feet and after a while he came back to Bishop John and said, "I've got a problem. You know for a while my tithe every week was a hundred dollars, but now it's triple that. I don't know what to do." What he meant was that he liked making three times the money, but he didn't like giving three times the tithe.

The Holy Spirit gave Bishop John just the right words to keep this man from getting his clothes dirty. He said, "I can fix that for you."

The man said, "You can?"

"Yes. I am going to pray that you'll go back to the income where you only had to pay $100.00 tithe. That'll fix it."

The man shook his head and said, "No! Don't do that!"

If I were to pick one area where most Christians get their divine clothes dirty, it would be finances. This is a hot topic because we need money to pay our bills and feed our families. Just the thought of not being able to provide for our basic needs scares people. On top of that, we often put our trust in money and get false security from having a lot of it. "If only I won the lottery, I would never have to worry about anything again." If that's true, why do most people who win the lottery end up losing it all and going right back to where they were financially? I believe it's because they didn't know God or trust Him. They put their faith and trust in money instead.

If God starts blessing you, He expects you to have enough maturity to at least give the ten percent tithe. If you are smart, you will give every time He gives you the opportunity. Then you can go to sleep at night knowing you have put your whole life in His capable hands. He is your God, not money.

Jesus said that money would be a great challenge to our flesh. He warned us that we cannot serve God and money:

> **No man can serve two masters: for either he will hate the one, and love the other; or else he will hold to the one, and despise the other. Ye cannot serve God and mammon.**
>
> Matthew 6:24

Mammon means wealth and riches. You have a choice to either be clothed in dollar bills or in the righteousness of God in Christ Jesus. Which do you think will love you, protect you, and give you the desires of your heart?

Jesus presented mammon as a spiritual being that opposes God and uses wealth and riches to tempt and destroy God's people. If we read on in Matthew 6:25-33, Jesus goes on to say how God takes care of us and He instructs us to seek first His kingdom and righteousness. That's why tithing and giving offerings as the Lord leads us is so important. It's another powerful way to show that we've got our divine clothes on.

When you make a decision about how you are going to make money or spend money, be sure you are seeking first God's kingdom and righteousness. That will keep you financially safe and sound. Remember Jesus' warning that choosing to serve mammon will cause you to resent and even hate God when He asks you to give. Eventually, love of mammon will destroy you.

The answer to our problems is never money; the answer is always Jesus Christ. When you seek Him and make right choices in your financial dealings, He will add everything you need in abundance.

Dressed for Favor

Have you ever noticed that when you are dressed appropriately for where you're going, you have confidence? If you're not dressed correctly, you feel unsteady and unsure. Having the right clothes on means a lot in the natural, and it means everything in the spirit. The world says to "dress for success," and they got that right. Your clothes say a lot about who you are, what you think about yourself, and whether you honor the people you are with.

When you know you're dressed right, you will have favor with other people.

> For thou, Lord, wilt bless the righteous; with favour wilt thou compass him as with a shield.
>
> **Psalm 5:12**

The Lord blesses those who make right choices. He surrounds them with divine favor, which is like a supernatural defense shield. God loves you just the way you are and when He showers His favor on you, other people love you just the way you are, too. When you walk into a room, confidently dressed in your divine robe of righteousness, humbly putting all your faith and trust in God, He inspires everyone in that room to have faith and trust in you. That's how favor works.

Favor works through your confidence or faith in God. This faith falters and fails if you don't have a clear conscience. How do you keep a clear conscience before God? The Word acts as a lamp to your feet and light to your pathway, showing you the right way to go (Psalm 119:105). Jesus said in John 14:6 that your Comforter, the Holy Spirit, would "teach you all things." He will teach you everything you need to know in any moment and any situation. The Word and the Spirit let you know what is the right decision and when you make right choices, you keep your conscience clear.

Your conscience is where your spirit tells you what is right and wrong. It's where you know what is ethical, moral, and true. When your conscience is clear, your confidence is fully in God and He can bless you and give you favor. It's wonderful to have a clear conscience! There is such freedom and joy, and God's infinite possibilities open up to you.

Judson Cornwall, a wonderful man of God who is now in Heaven with the Lord, demonstrated this concept in a very public way. He was in a church in Philadelphia and there had been a lot of preliminaries. When they took up the offering, the Lord said to him, "Put in $10.00."

Brother Cornwall said, "Well, Lord, I've only got a $5.00 bill, a $10.00 bill, and a $1.00 bill." The offering basket came by, and he put the $5.00 bill in. He figured that was enough for the guest minister to give. As he began to preach, there was just no anointing or life in his words. In his mind, Brother Cornwall asked the Lord what was the matter, and the Lord told him to repent. He stopped preaching and said, "Whoever has the offering plate, come here, please." He reached in his pocket and pulled out the $10.00 bill. Now that his conscience was clear, God's anointing, His favor and blessing, flowed through his message.

Later Brother Cornwall said, "If you're not feeling victory in your life, if God is not answering your prayers and if you haven't got peace when you lay your head down, if things are not going right for you and you're a believer, then stop and go back and do the last thing God told you to do that you didn't do."

Remember Proverbs 16:7? When your ways please the Lord, he will give you such favor that even your enemies will be at peace with you. First John 5:14 says that when you pray according to God's will, you have confidence that He hears your prayers, and if He hears them, He answers them.

There have been times when I have been praying so fervently, and then I sense a check in my spirit. I realize I'm praying my will—giving God ultimatums and telling Him exactly what He should do—and have forgotten to seek first His righteousness. Immediately I will say, "Lord, please erase everything I just said! I only want Your will." Then my conscience is clear, I can pray according to His will in confidence, and His favor comes all over me.

A troubled conscience means something is trying to get your royal robes dirty! If there are things in your past that still torment you, ask the Holy Spirit to show you the way to freedom. Ask God to forgive you or ask somebody else to forgive you if you need to, but close the door on the wrong choices of the past. If you have been wounded, let it go. Forgiveness is not a feeling; forgiveness is a choice. When you choose to forgive, you put yourself in God's hands so He can heal you. If you don't forgive, you imprison yourself in torment.

When you refuse to forgive, your conscience condemns you because you are not being like Jesus. He forgave you on the cross, and you put Him there! Choose to be like Jesus and forgive those who hurt you. Get back into your divine clothes and be free!

Delight to Be Right

For if our heart condemn us, God is greater than our heart, and knoweth all things.

Beloved, if our heart condemn us not, then have we confidence toward God.

And whatsoever we ask, we receive of him, because we keep his commandments, and do those things that are pleasing in his sight.

1 John 3:20-22

Be happy and delight to do the will of God. If your heart condemns you, God is greater! Turn to Him and He will tell you what you need to do to clear your conscience and restore your confidence. Keep His commandments by obeying His Word and His Spirit. The Word and the Spirit will always agree. I've heard people say things like, "Well, the Holy Spirit told me that my wife is just not treating me right, and He has brought this other woman into my life so that I can be happy." The Holy Spirit is not going to say something that is against the commandments of the Lord, and the commandment clearly says, "Thou shalt not commit adultery" (Exodus 20:14). That message they think they're hearing is most definitely not from the Holy Spirit!

God's Spirit will always speak according to God's Word. To keep your conscience clear and remain happy and free in God's favor and blessing, your greatest delight must be in pleasing Him. Believe me, I've lived with a clear conscience and a troubled conscience, and a clear conscience is better in every way!

You know what it's like when you take a bath or a shower, wash your hair, and your whole body is clean and smelling good. That's what your spirit became when the Holy Spirit regenerated it. You became clean and fresh and a brand-new creation in Christ Jesus. That's why God put His robe of righteousness on you. He gave you a suit of clothes that reflects the fact that you are His beloved child.

When you are tempted to sin, Satan is trying to get you to dump a bucket of the foulest smelling stuff all over your clean, white clothes. Whether it's greed, lust, or pride, it's the wrong choice, and it will make you feel dirty. After that, only repentance—turning away from sin and back to God—will clear your conscience and restore your soul to its beautiful, divine clothes.

You are dressed by God to make right choices. When you walk into a room, you should hear the swish of your royal robe and feel the weight of that royal diadem on your head. That's a reminder to keep your thinking straight! With the understanding of who you are in Christ Jesus, you won't consider getting your clothes dirty. You never want to dishonor your King or your brothers and sisters in the Lord.

Let your divine clothes shine in His glory!

11

The Sons of God

One evening when I was first married, Bishop John told me he was going to bring a lot of the young people to our house for dinner and fellowship. I didn't really know how to cook, but I was determined to fix something for supper. I boiled a pot of rice and made chili from a package, thinking we would put the chili on the rice. It all looked good until John and the kids didn't come when they were supposed to. The rice was getting cold and I didn't know whether rice could be warmed up later, so I poured the chili over the rice and put the lid back on the pot to keep everything warm.

When Bishop John came home, he took the lid off the pot and saw that the mixture was up to the top. He said, "What is this?"

I said, "I don't know, but eat it before it gets any bigger!"

Just like the rice expanded in that pot, that is the way I feel about this revelation of righteousness God has given me. It just keeps getting bigger and bigger, so I hope you are eating it up as we go along! I promise you, it will do what good spiritual food does; it will cause you to grow and mature in God.

The Bible says the whole creation is longing for the manifestation of the mature sons and daughters of God (Romans 8:19).

What does a mature Christian look like and sound like? First of all, they make right choices to keep from being deceived.

Let No Man Deceive You

Little children, let no man deceive you: he that doeth righteousness is righteous, even as he is righteous.

He that committeth sin is of the devil; for the devil sinneth from the beginning. For this purpose the Son of God was manifested, that he might destroy the works of the devil.

Whosoever is born of God doth not commit sin; for his seed remaineth in him: and he cannot sin, because he is born of God.

In this the children of God are manifest, and the children of the devil: whosoever doeth not righteousness is not of God, neither he that loveth not his brother.

For this is the message that ye heard from the beginning, that we should love one another.

1 John 3:7-11

You can't get around this! The Word of God says that the children of God are manifest, or recognized, by the fact that they make right choices. In other words, they don't sin.

John says, "Don't be deceived by anything the devil, the world, or your natural thinking might tell you: You are righteous to make right choices. You are to reject sin and obey God. Then you destroy the works of the devil and love others the way Jesus loves you."

As I was reading and studying the Scriptures, it came to me that everywhere I saw the word *evil*, I could put in *unrighteousness*; and everywhere I saw the word *good*, I could put in *righteous*. Using this as a key, more scriptures began to open up to me.

Having a good conscience; that, whereas they speak evil [unrighteously] of you, as of evildoers [unrighteous], they may be ashamed that falsely accuse your good [righteous] conversation in Christ.

1 Peter 3:16 [inserts mine]

Your *conversation* is your lifestyle, behavior, and conduct. When you are righteous and making decisions to please the Lord, those who are unrighteous will often speak evil of you. This is not pleasant! But it is better to be seeking first God's righteousness and to have a clear conscience than to be guilty of what you're being accused of doing. Suffering in the will of God means you are not enduring alone. Jesus, who suffered for you, is right there with you to strengthen you and give you the courage to continue making right choices.

If you are sinning and people are talking about it, you have no defense. All you can do is humble yourself, repent, and do what needs to be done to set things right. But Peter is saying that if you are making right choices, anyone who speaks against you will end up being ashamed. When you hear their accusations, your conscience will be clear, and you can trust God to clear your name.

Beloved, follow not that which is evil [unrighteous, wrong choices], but that which is good [righteous, right choices].

He that doeth good [righteous, right choices] is of God: but he that doeth evil [unrighteous, wrong choices] hath not seen God.

3 John 11 [inserts mine]

If you do good and make right choices, you are of God. If you do evil and make wrong choices, you are not of God. Those are strong words the mature believer must take very seriously. Mature believers cannot conduct their lives just any way they want and remain strong in the Lord. If they continually give in to temptation and sin, if they entertain ideas and images of the world, then they can easily be deceived and think they're okay when they are not. Mature Christians are rarely deceived in this way because they realize they have to abide in God's Word and obey the Holy Spirit to stay okay. Staying close to God and His people will keep them from being deceived.

Love and Truth

For the earnest expectation of the creature waiteth for the manifestation of the sons of God.

For the creature was made subject to vanity, not willingly, but by reason of him who hath subjected the same in hope,

because the creature itself also shall be delivered from the bondage of corruption into the glorious liberty of the children of God.

Romans 8:19-21

All of creation, every creature in the earth that labors under the curse of sin, is waiting for the manifestation—the revealing, the coming into reality—of the sons of God. The Greek word translated "sons" in verse 19 denotes maturity. The Bible speaks of babes in Christ and those who are mature in Christ. The world is waiting in eager anticipation to see just what a mature son or daughter of God looks like, speaks like, and acts like.

Mature Christians are often hard to find. That's sad, but it's the truth. We should want to mature in Christ because as we grow up in Him, we experience glorious liberty in God. Liberty means freedom! However, true liberty is living as we should and not as we please. Too many believers still want to live as they please.

We all know right from wrong. Even a little baby knows right from wrong. When my granddaughter Asia was eight months old, she was sitting next to my purse one Sunday morning during the church service. She put her hand inside my purse, and then she looked up at me. She didn't go any further. I thought, *She doesn't know if she should be doing that.* After the service, my glasses were in my hand, and she reached over, took them, and put them on. Then she looked at me as if to ask, "Are you going to take the glasses away from me? Am I doing something wrong?"

At eight months of age, Asia's conscience was working. She knew there is a difference between right and wrong and she wanted to know if what she was doing was right. Sometimes I wish Christians would wake up and want to know the same thing! A whole lot more of us would come to maturity if we were seeking first God's righteousness and doing what is right.

My passion is to teach God's people how to grow up to become more like Jesus. As Asia's grandmother, I have the same commission from the Lord. Asia's family must teach her the difference between right and wrong, giving her the truth of God's Word and instructing her in how to hear and obey the Holy Spirit.

For as many as are led by the Spirit of God, they are the sons of God.

Romans 8:14

Who are the sons of God? The definition is clear and plain in this scripture—the sons of God are those who are led by the Spirit. From the moment you are born again and the Spirit of God comes into your spirit, you can hear Him. Sometimes He speaks the Word of God. Sometimes He speaks in words, instructing you, encouraging you, or correcting you. Sometimes He just gives you a nudge, an impression, or an inclination to do or say this or that. Even when He is deadly serious and stern, there is a gentleness about Him. He always speaks the truth in love.

The world is crying out for love and truth, and you are the one to reveal them! But it takes some maturity, which only comes from being led by the Holy Spirit.

Following the Spirit

It takes time for us to recognize when and how the Holy Spirit is speaking to us and thankfully, He is patient—much more patient than we are! But after a few years, if we have been earnestly seeking first God's kingdom and His righteousness, we should be well on our way to knowing when the Holy Spirit is leading us.

Verily, verily, I say unto you, The Son can do nothing of himself, but what he seeth the Father do: for what things soever he doeth, these also doeth the Son likewise.

122

I can of mine own self do nothing: as I hear, I judge: and my judgment is just; because I seek not mine own will, but the will of the Father which hath sent me.

John 5:19,30

How do you think Jesus saw the Father doing things? How did He receive wisdom and power? The Holy Spirit! Jesus was *the* mature Son of God, and He did everything by the Spirit and the Word of God.

One of the things we learn as we grow into maturity is that we can grieve the Holy Spirit by not allowing Him to lead us and change us. When we go against God's Word, we can feel His grief and disappointment inside us. This also happens when we think about, say, or do things that displease the Lord.

Years ago, Bishop John and I were in New York. We had been told there was a Broadway play we would enjoy, so we got tickets and went. We were sitting up close and by the time they got through the first part of the show, John looked at me and said, "Let's get out of here." As soon as we could, we got up and walked out the back door. Something in that show grieved us, and we recognized the leading of the Holy Spirit. He was saying, "This is not for you."

This is another way the Holy Spirit leads you: by conviction of sin (John 16:8). For example, let's say you are on your way to have dinner with a man who is not your husband, and you are convicted that what you are doing is wrong. Your spirit is not at peace; in fact, you are in turmoil inside. The Holy Spirit is convicting you of sin. Maybe you are thinking of lying to save your own skin, but inside your spirit is churning. The Holy Spirit is convicting you of sin.

When you obey the conviction of the Holy Spirit, you are being led of Him. Mature believers know that you don't grow up in God by sinning habitually. Even the most mature might fall into sin now and then, but they are quick to repent and close all doors that would lead them to sin again. They know that they can't be intimate with God and have sin in their lives.

When you respond to the Spirit's conviction, you are growing in maturity, and He is keeping your conscience clear and your slate clean. He is keeping you on the right path, in the right place at the right time. I call it divine radar.

The Holy Spirit wants to lead us in the right paths. Let's say you start out going to work, and you have this desire to stop and get coffee at a convenience store—something you never do. When you walk in, you see a man leaning against the drink cabinet. He is obviously in great distress. The Holy Spirit focuses your attention on him, so you walk over and ask if you can help him. You end up praying for him, telling him about Jesus, and walk out of that store with a new disciple in the Lord!

Have you ever gone somewhere and thought, *I don't know why I'm doing this?* When you arrived, you found out exactly why the Holy Spirit led you to that place. Sometimes He might tell you, "Go to this corner and turn." Why are you turning? You don't know. Just turn because He said turn. I'd rather err on the side of listening and obeying than to ignore the Holy Spirit's promptings, grieve Him, and miss God's will.

To be *led* means *directed, governed, and guided by the Spirit of God.* Those who are led by the Spirit of God are the sons of God. I have often wondered how many believers were prompted to stay home from work or were delayed in getting to work just before the World Trade Center bombing September 11, 2001. There are many stories of those who were spared this way.

We never know what the Holy Spirit is saving us from, so we have to take Him seriously even when it is something small. Did you get ready to step out the door and just have a prompting, "Go get the umbrella." You look outside and it's sunny, so you don't take the umbrella. Later, it starts pouring down rain and you get drenched. You look and feel terrible by the time you arrive at your meeting.

When this has happened to me, I've asked, "Lord, why didn't I get it?"

He said, "Well, I'll keep telling you and pretty soon, you'll figure out that it's Me talking to you. After a while, you'll learn to do what I tell you to do, because you will have experienced what happens when you don't."

Being led is not just hearing; it is also obeying. You're not led if you're not doing what the Holy Spirit told you to do. The more you listen and obey, the more times you make the right choice, the more you will grow up into a mature son or daughter of God.

The Age of Maturity

In the Bible, the age of maturity is thirty. Jesus began His ministry when He was thirty; Joseph told Pharaoh the meaning of his dream and began to rule in Egypt when he was thirty; David became king of Israel at thirty; and priests in the Tabernacle and the Temple began to serve when they were thirty.

All of these men had a lot of experiences and did a lot of significant things before they were thirty, but God knew they were mature enough to step into their actual purpose when they were thirty. They had made enough right choices and gone through enough trials and temptations to succeed in their callings.

As they ministered to the Lord, and fasted, the Holy Ghost said, Separate me Barnabas and Saul for the work whereunto I have called them.

Acts 13:2

No one knew the Old Testament Scriptures, which were the only Scriptures at the time of Jesus, better than Saul of Tarsus. Nevertheless, after he got saved in Acts, chapter 9, there were several chapters and a lot of years before the Holy Spirit made him the apostle Paul and sent him out to preach the gospel and teach the Word.

There may not be a specific age God has picked as the point of maturity, but it is clear to me that it takes decades to reach maturity. Furthermore, once you reach maturity, you realize what you still don't know is overwhelming! This is another mark of maturity: You realize how much you still have to learn about God, about life in Him and all of His creation, about people, and about yourself.

Mature believers know that they don't know it all, but they can still have confidence in their future because they have intimate knowledge of the One who does. They make more and more right choices because their relationship with God is the most important relationship in their lives. They seek Him first in all things and make decisions according to His Word and His Spirit. That is why their lives have peace, stability, lots of fruit, and joy.

Faith and Humility

And we know that all things work together for good to them that love God, to them who are the called according to his purpose.

Romans 8:28

I looked up *work together* in Strong's Concordance, and one of the definitions was *to put forth power together with and thereby to assist.* God puts forth His supernatural power in all things to work them out for our good, for our righteousness. He does that for those who love Him and are fulfilling His purpose for their lives. After you see Him do this again and again over several decades of loving Him and serving Him, maturity just comes. Maturity is evidenced by a deeper faith and greater humility.

When you are a mature Christian, you know you can't do anything without God. You have more understanding and compassion for others, especially for the babes in Christ around you. One of the mistakes we make is assuming that because a believer is a couple of years old in the Lord and is full of zeal, they are mature. They are not! They need to be discipled just like all of us. Too many young believers are put in positions of authority too soon, which harms both them and the church. Read 1 Timothy, chapter 3, where Paul lists all the qualifications for leadership. Just reading this list causes me to hit my knees!

We need to give new believers time to learn the things of God and grow in the ways of God. When we put them in a position that is beyond their spiritual maturity, they can get puffed up in pride (1 Timothy 3:6), especially if they see some success. Then the devil comes in and destroys them through their pride, because pride always leads to a fall (Proverbs 16:18). They may be so devastated, that they'll turn away from God and/or the church and become bitter. We can't let that happen!

We need to teach new believers to seek first God's kingdom and His righteousness, and we need to demonstrate that in front of them by making godly choices and being honest about the consequences of any bad choices we've made. People generally know when you're being a hypocrite, so you better be honest.

We also need to prepare new Christians to face difficult times and understand how valuable these challenges can be if handled right. One of the things the Lord told me years ago was, "If you understood the purpose of the fiery trial, you would leap into it and embrace it."

I still have to confess, I have not yet found any trials I wanted to leap into and embrace! Nevertheless, I've gone through a couple of infernos where the Holy Spirit burned a lot of rubbish out of me. Afterward, I felt like a bird let out of a cage! That's what I tell young believers. I encourage them and give them hope as they go through their fiery trials. There is a greater good to gain, so be humble and have faith! As they make right choices, God is working it all together for their good and bringing them to maturity.

> **But the natural man receiveth not the things of the Spirit of God: for they are foolishness unto him: neither can he know them, because they are spiritually discerned.**
>
> **1 Corinthians 2:14**

The world thinks it knows what it needs, but it doesn't. Deep inside the heart of every human being is a burning desire to know who they are, what their purpose is, and that they are cherished and loved by their Father God. Jesus is the only one who can fill that hole in their heart, and so they are crying out for the manifestation of the sons of God. We should be living, breathing examples of what it means to really know God, be a part of His family, and know who we are in Him.

God wants us to grow into maturity so we can be His witnesses to a lost and dying world, the world Jesus died to save. We can show them the way to glory!

12

The Way to Glory

The Spirit itself beareth witness with our spirit, that we are the children of God:

and if children, then heirs; heirs of God, and joint-heirs with Christ; if so be that we suffer with him, that we may be also glorified together.

For I reckon that the sufferings of this present time are not worthy to be compared with the glory which shall be revealed in us.

For the earnest expectation of the creature waiteth for the manifestation of the sons of God.

Romans 8:16-19

You know in your spirit that you are a child of God; and if you are His child, then you are His heir and joint-heir with Jesus Christ. In simple terms, that means that with Jesus and through Jesus, all God's blessings and benefits are yours.

I want you to notice that the second part of verse 17 begins with an *if*. It says, "if so be that we suffer with him."

What did Jesus tell us? "If any man will come after me, let him deny himself, and take up his cross daily, and follow me" (Luke 9:23). Can you do that? Have you been doing that? Making right choices means crucifying your flesh to follow the Lord. This is very painful at times but we have a joy set before us: If we suffer as Jesus did, we will be glorified with Him.

Verse 18 talks about "the sufferings of this present time," which are our afflictions, misfortunes, calamities, and growing pains. The Word says these things are not worthy to be compared with the glory revealed in us. What is this glory that is revealed in us? The manifested presence of God—His grace and His goodness flowing through every right choice we make. All our fiery trials and tribulations amount to nothing compared with the pure gold of God's honor and power that shines through our lives.

The path to glory is littered with all the rubbish you put to death as you made every decision to seek God's kingdom and His righteousness. In the end, there might not be much left of the old you, but what is left is pure gold. The best part is that all along the way, you won't have suffered alone. Jesus was right there with you.

Growing Pains

What I am saying is that as long as an heir is underage, he is no different from a slave, although he owns the whole estate. The heir is subject to guardians and trustees until the time set by his father.

Galatians 4:1-2 NIV

In these verses, Paul tells us that an heir may be the benefi-
ciary of all of his father's wealth, but until he is of age—which is
decided by the father—he is under the control of teachers and
instructors. Little Asia is almost one year old, and she is one of
my heirs. She's an heir of everything I have, but as long as she's
a baby, she's under "tutors and governors" (as the King James
Version would say) until she reaches maturity. When we first are
saved, we are just babes. We need teachers, trainers, coaches, and
overseers who are preparing us for what God is calling us to do.

> **Wherefore he saith, When he ascended up on high, he led
> captivity captive, and gave gifts unto men.**
>
> **And he gave some, apostles; and some, prophets; and some,
> evangelists; and some, pastors and teachers;**
>
> **for the perfecting of the saints, for the work of the ministry,
> for the edifying of the body of Christ:**
>
> **Ephesians 4:8, 11-12**

God wants us to grow up. He wants us to become as He is.
We are not to remain immature, lusting for forbidden things,
giving into our flesh. He wants us to learn from all the gifts He's
given us: the apostles, prophets, evangelists, pastors, and teachers
He places us under. They teach us, train us, encourage us, and
correct us so that we make more and more right choices.

I was praying for someone who was in a lifestyle that was not
godly, and the Holy Spirit said to me, "I don't call anything sin
that doesn't involve a choice." God won't hold you responsible
and say you sinned if you did something without knowing it was
sin. If a person was born into a family that did drugs and that
child grew up thinking that being drunk or high was normal,
then God wouldn't hold that sin against them. But once that

person hears the truth, she has to make a choice to obey the truth or not. That's when God holds her responsible.

The person I was praying for knew what the Bible said, and the person had chosen to sin. That's why I was interceding for the individual, for the Holy Spirit to convict the person and for his or her heart to turn back to the Lord. Too many believers know what the Word says, but they want what they want. They have an ungodly desire and they find ways to justify acting on it. As soon as an opportunity to sin presents itself, they go with it. Sin is a choice.

Crucifying our flesh is harder than anything else in the Christian walk. This is where we experience the worst growing pains. I think this is because we don't want to think that we have a weakness or wicked desires. Some believers refuse to face their faults because their pride gets in the way. They just can't stand the idea that they have a problem, especially a sin problem. If they are going to grow up, it may involve some pain; but in the end, they will love the freedom they have in the Lord.

Sometimes we just don't want to come to grips with what the Word says about something because it goes against what the world is telling us is right. We avoid the issue until we have to make a decision. Are we going to submit to the truth of God's Word and line up our life with it, or are we going to twist the Word to fit what we want? Making our flesh conform to the Word instead of the world is a big growing pain!

Then there's the devil. The truth is, if you're making right choices in line with God's Word and Spirit, you are in position to cast out any evil spirit sent your way. James 4:7 says: "Submit yourselves therefore to God. Resist the devil, and he will flee from you." Make the right choice to submit to the Word and the

Holy Spirit. Resist the devil's lies, wiles, deceptions, distractions, and temptations, then watch him flee.

Iron Sharpens Iron

Ephesians 4:11-12 says Jesus gave five ministry gifts for the perfecting or maturing of the saints, so we can minister to each other and be salt and light to the world. The word "perfect" means mature; it doesn't mean every choice you make is exactly right, but almost!

> Till we all come in the unity of the faith, and of the knowledge of the Son of God, unto a perfect man, unto the measure of the stature of the fulness of Christ.
>
> Ephesians 4:13

> Jesus is the head, and we are His body. We don't want Him to sit on a scrawny, ignorant, wimpy body. We want to be strong and wise so we can honor Him and carry out His will.

> That we henceforth be no more children, tossed to and fro, and carried about with every wind of doctrine, by the sleight of men, and cunning craftiness, whereby they lie in wait to deceive.
>
> Ephesians 4:14

This is so important! In the last chapter, we talked about what mature believers look like. Mature believers are not deceived. They don't go after all kinds of wild ideas that have nothing to do with what the Word of God says. They stick to the Word and follow the Spirit. That's how they become mature and stay strong in the Lord.

Some believers just want to go from one healing miracle meeting to another. They want the power. We should all want to walk in God's power, but God says, "You know, there's more to Me than that. If you don't study My Word and grow up, you're going to be tossed to and fro like children. You are going to be ashamed (2 Timothy 2:15) and embarrass yourself because you don't know what My Word really says."

I see people go from church to church, and they never grow any roots. They're like tumbleweeds that just roll around, leaving a lot of dust and no fruit. They go here and there, blown about by "every wind of doctrine," by any crazy teaching that's being thrown out there.

> But speaking the truth in love, may grow up into him in all things, which is the head, even Christ.
>
> **Ephesians 4:15**

Grow up! Have you ever said that to your child, a friend, or even your spouse? The Word tells us to choose to become like Jesus, to be worthy of our Head by becoming His mature body.

> But when that which is perfect is come, then that which is in part shall be done away.
>
> When I was a child, I spake as a child, I understood as a child, I thought as a child: but when I became a man, I put away childish things.
>
> **1 Corinthians 13:10-11**

Selfishness is probably the root of everything that is childish. It shows itself in what you speak, how you think, and what you do. Children haven't learned to seek first God's kingdom and His righteousness. They say whatever comes into their minds, their imaginations run wild, and they usually throw a tantrum if they can't do what they want to do or get what they want.

Unfortunately, many Christians who have been born again for years are still acting this way.

Growing up is an individual process, but it can't happen apart from the body of Christ. A believer who doesn't go to church is usually a very immature believer. We don't grow up by watching Christian television in our recliners at home. We grow up when we serve the Lord alongside other people.

Iron sharpeneth iron; so a man sharpeneth the countenance of his friend.

Proverbs 27:17

You don't want to be a dull blade! You want to be sharp and wise and full of God's love and truth. This happens when you choose not to forsake the assembling of the saints (Hebrews 10:25), learn from the five-fold gifts Jesus places in your life, and obey the Word and the Spirit in order to get along with others. As you do these things, you will grow up and experience the joy of accomplishing His will for your life while helping your brothers and sisters realize their dreams too.

The Lord's been talking to me a whole lot about watching what I say, think, and feel in my heart. More than ever, I'm trying to be careful not to judge anybody in an unrighteous, ungodly way. He said, "You'll be a whole lot healthier in your spirit, soul, and body if you regard the words of your mouth, because out of the abundance of your heart, your mouth is speaking." Many times a day I say to myself, "I don't need to say that. I don't need to be thinking about this. My feelings need to line up and be at peace."

I was on the phone with a friend who was expressing how very distressed she was over a presidential election. She was almost frantic, and I blurted out, "No, wait! Watch your attitude. Watch what you're saying. Don't sin with your attitude." Later I wondered if I should have said that. I realized I had reacted to her fear without seeking first God's righteousness.

> **But why dost thou judge thy brother? or why dost thou set at nought thy brother? for we shall all stand before the judgment seat of Christ.**
>
> **Romans 14:10**

I have learned that if I choose to express frustration or anger at someone, I'm sinning with my mouth. God doesn't want me to harbor anger or fear in my heart because they lead to a critical spirit. It's normal for a believer to be upset and alarmed when they see someone making wrong choices; it's not normal for a mature son or daughter of God to act out of anger or fear. We are to trust God. He is the answer, and losing our temper or worrying will only make the situation worse.

Mature believers learn to consider others before themselves. They let God deal with their issues so they can pray, forgive, and obey what the Holy Spirit and the Word command them to do regarding their brother or sister. They walk in truth and love, giving honor and glory to the Lord in everything.

I finally said to my friend who was so upset over the election, "Don't let the enemy bring a spirit of harassment and frustration upon you. That's not God. This is in God's hands, and we're going to pray and believe Him for what He wants, because He's in charge. Nobody's told me God went on vacation!" Iron sharpened iron, we both grew up a little, and we were both blessed.

Nobody Gets Away with Anything

We're not supposed to be critical and judgmental toward each other, but we can judge sin when we see it. One day I asked the Lord, "Why does that person get away with that? I can't do that."

The Lord answered, "Nobody gets away with anything."

And as it is appointed unto men once to die, but after this the judgment.

Hebrews 9:27

But I say unto you, That every idle word that men shall speak, they shall give account thereof in the day of judgment.

Matthew 12:36

The Bible talks about judgment in our everyday lives, but it also talks about a Day of Judgment, when each one of us will give an account for the life we lived and the choices we made. On that Day, you can't say, "The devil made me do it," or "My friends pressured me." The Day of Judgment is just between you and Jesus, and you are responsible for every decision you made. A mature believer understands and accepts this, and tries to make right choices. That believer can live in peace and have a bold confidence about giving an account before the Lord.

Herein is our love made perfect, that we may have boldness in the day of judgment: because as he is, so are we in this world.

1 John 4:17

If we are growing up in Christ Jesus, we can remain confident that we will be okay when we stand before Him. We want Him to say, "Well done, thou good and faithful servant" (Matthew 25:21). We don't want Him to say, "What were you thinking?!!!"

When you're dealing with a child who doesn't know that what he or she did was wrong, you teach him God's Word and instruct him in making right choices. If he does it again, he is in rebellion to God as well as you, so out comes the rod. The rod doesn't bruise, but it stings. It makes the point that sin causes pain, and no one gets away with sin.

As that child grows older and as the Word and the Spirit are working in him, he will become mature and realize that even if no one sees, sin will cause him pain. Mature believers avoid sin like the plague. They have learned that even though sin may be pleasurable for a season, in the end it will ruin their lives. They know they can't really get away with anything!

The Ministry of the Saints

And he gave some, apostles; and some, prophets; and some, evangelists; and some, pastors and teachers;

for the perfecting of the saints, for the work of the ministry, for the edifying of the body of Christ:

Ephesians 4:11-12

Who is supposed to be doing the work of the ministry? The saints! The five gifts are like gardening tools that you need to have a fruitful garden. You need a hand cultivator to break up the soil and prepare it. That's like the apostles and prophets, who build the foundation of your faith. They plant churches and establish ministries, then keep them on the straight and narrow in the areas of doctrine and expanding the kingdom of God. You also need a spade to dig the hole in which you'll plant the seed or place the young plant. That's like the preachers and evangelists, who bring in the new believers.

Once the seeds or plants are in place (new believers), then you need to have a watering can to hydrate the soil, one of those gardening weeders to keep the weeds out, and shears to prune the plants as they grow. These would be like the pastors and teachers who instruct you in how to live by the Spirit and the Word in everyday life.

Even when a garden has all this attention, it can still fail. If a garden doesn't get enough sunlight, it will fail and so will a believer who doesn't receive and obey all the revelation given to them by the Son through His ministry gifts and His body. This revelation is how God nourishes a believer, deals with sin issues, and keeps him on the right path making right choices.

This process is going to continue "Till we all come in the unity of the faith, and of the knowledge of the Son of God, unto a perfect man, unto the measure of the stature of the fulness of Christ" (Ephesians 4:13). One day we are going to flow together in faith as one body, and it's going to be so glorious that people will say, "Look at the Church! They are just like Jesus!"

We're going to know Him, not just know about Him.

We're going to obey Him when we hear His command.

We're going to demonstrate His miracle-working power.

We're going to manifest His honor and integrity.

We're going to speak the truth of His Word in love.

The way to glory is the Church making right choices!

13

....

The Power Is Yours

If I went to a prison and interviewed the inmates, asking them why they were there, they would say, "Well, I committed this crime."

"Would you consider that you made a bad choice? Is that why you're here?"

"Well, yes."

Moving to the next cell, I'd ask, "Excuse me. Why are you on death row? Could you say it was all your bad choices?"

"Yes, ma'am."

How many interviews would I need to do to find someone who would say, "I'm here because I made great choices in life"?

We must wake up! There are consequences when we do things our way and thumb our noses at God. When our choices have led us down a path of trouble, we cry out to God and say,

"I need my rent paid. Please heal me. Help me get what I want." Then when He doesn't answer with a blessing, we blame God.

There's something wrong when believers are not being blessed by the Lord; God does not suddenly decide to be stingy, selfish, and uncaring. No, that sounds more like believers who have never disciplined themselves to seek first His kingdom and His righteousness. When believers are not being blessed by the Lord, it's probably because they didn't make right choices and are now reaping the consequences, which are frustrating and sometimes tragic.

I have a constant reminder of this truth because I fight diabetes. My blood sugar rises or falls according to what I eat. I experience almost instant consequences to my choices. If I choose to eat healthy, then I feel good; if I choose to eat anything I want, I feel bad and might even become dangerously ill.

One day I checked my blood sugar and it was very high. I said out loud, "How did this happen?"

A gentle voice inside said, "Well, it was the chocolate sundae, the ham sandwich, and the Coke." I was caught! There were no excuses. My sugar was up because I made some bad choices. The consequences I experience are not just high blood sugar but also the deterioration of the organs of my body. As a diabetic, how I feel as well as how long I live are determined by my own choices.

Before you start feeling sorry for me, consider this: Whether it is what you feed your body or your spirit, you decide your future by the choices you make today. God has given you the right to choose your destiny, and you can do it His way or your way. If you read and study His Word, you quickly realize that His way is best!

Godly Strength

The people that do know their God shall be strong, and do exploits.

Daniel 11:32

The world is waiting for believers who will live under the absolute authority and dominion of the Lord Jesus Christ. These Christians know that their internal life determines their external life. Did you know that every thought triggers an emotion, and people are more inclined to speak or act a certain way because of an emotion rather than a rational thought? Emotional experiences go deep into our hearts and affect how we react to circumstances. That's why God exhorts us again and again to guard our hearts (Proverbs 4:23).

We talk about *strength of character*, which means controlling our emotions by focusing our thoughts on God's kingdom and His righteousness. When we discipline ourselves to think right, we keep a godly check on our emotions and draw upon God's strength to make the right choices.

When you dwell on lustful, proud, greedy, angry, hateful, or scary thoughts, it causes corresponding emotions that affect your body in a negative way and can make you sick or cause you to say or do things you will regret later. On the other hand, when you think on the Lord and renew your mind with His Word, the Holy Spirit lights you up with revelation and peace. He is able to impart to you the supernatural strength you need to do great exploits for the Lord. Do you see that His power is yours when you make the right choices?

> **Flee also youthful lusts: but follow righteousness, faith, charity, peace, with them that call on the Lord out of a pure heart.**
>
> 2 Timothy 2:22

Young people have to be trained to discipline themselves, and so do young believers. Before we are saved, we go after anything we want. A child and a young person are often consumed with getting what they want. Have you been to the grocery store lately? These days, you can't go shopping without hearing a child throwing a fit because the parent won't get the child what he or she wants. If they continue to act like that as an adult, they will have a terrible life.

I'm sure some of the multitude followed Jesus for the loaves and the fishes. How many people did He heal, who never received Him as Lord and Savior? Do you know what that implies? Many followed Him for the miracles and to get their own needs met, to satisfy their "youthful lusts." But the ones who loved Him, followed Him and obeyed His Word. They drew upon His strength to overcome their youthful lusts and grow into maturity.

Jesus said in Matthew 6:21 that your heart is where your treasure is. In other words, whatever you love most in life is going to direct your life choices. If you have never disciplined your youthful lusts, then your heart is selfish. All your choices are based on getting your needs met. On the other hand, if your heart is with Jesus, all your choices are going to be based on pleasing Him. Proverbs 10:2 says that is a good thing, because treasures of wickedness (self-centeredness) profit nothing, but righteousness (right choices in line with God's will) delivers you from death.

You need look no further than the divorce rate in the church to know that believers are not fleeing youthful lusts. I know some people have scriptural grounds and good reason for divorce because of continual sexual immorality and physical abuse that puts the entire family in danger. But the truth is, most divorces are caused by a lack of maturity and a refusal to grow up in the Lord. The man and woman simply want what they want and they choose to serve themselves instead of honoring the covenant they made with both God and their spouse. They please themselves instead of God, and the idea of laying their lives down for their mate doesn't even cross their minds.

Making choices to satisfy youthful lusts is never going to make you happy or successful. You will never be satisfied, content, or at peace. Pleasures of unrighteousness, or wrong choices, benefit nothing. But right choices will rescue you, save you, and make you strong in the Lord and in the power of His might. Those who have His strength are the ones who will do great exploits. They are the ones who will have tremendous adventures of faith.

A Mighty Tree

Blessed is the man that walketh not in the counsel of the ungodly, nor standeth in the way of sinners, nor sitteth in the seat of the scornful.

But his delight is in the law of the Lord; and in his law doth he meditate day and night.

And he shall be like a tree planted by the rivers of water, that bringeth forth his fruit in his season; his leaf also shall not wither; and whatsoever he doeth shall prosper.

Psalm 1:1-3

Are you living like a mighty tree or a mouse? Are you prospering in whatever you pursue or are you hiding in holes to keep the cat from devouring you? The keys to a better quality of life are walking with the Lord and with His people, drinking in the refreshing, illuminating water of His Word, and bringing forth the fruit of the Holy Spirit.

Believers who are serious about living the abundant life Jesus died to give them are going to learn to embrace obedience and hate rebellion.

And having in a readiness to revenge all disobedience, when your obedience is fulfilled.

2 Corinthians 10:6

We must be ready to "revenge all unrighteousness." The moment we realize we made a wrong choice, we must repent. We must turn around and make the right choice. When we submit to right choices, our obedience will be fulfilled. We will have success and satisfaction. The choice may be hard to make, but we will breathe a sigh of relief when we find ourselves standing like mighty trees of divine strength in the face of danger, tragedy, or demonic attacks. In the power of the Holy Spirit, we are able to accomplish things we never imagined.

Knowing Christ

Yea doubtless, and I count all things but loss for the excellency of the knowledge of Christ Jesus my Lord: for whom I have suffered the loss of all things, and do count them but dung, that I may win Christ,

and be found in him, not having mine own righteousness, which is of the law, but that which is through the faith of Christ, the righteousness which is of God by faith.

Philippians 3:8-9

Paul said that everything was worthless next to knowing Christ Jesus. He didn't care that he lost everything he had achieved as a Pharisee, because under the Law he was continually frustrated. Paul tried to make himself righteous by making right choices to obey the law. But when he put his faith in Christ Jesus, *God's* righteousness was imparted to him, which was infinitely better than his own! When he became the righteousness of God in Christ Jesus, he received God's supernatural ability and power to make right choices.

Paul expressed his greatest desire when he said,

That I may know him, and the power of his resurrection, and the fellowship of his sufferings.

Philippians 3:10

This is the truth we need to embrace! If we suffer for the moment and make the right choice, if we pick up our cross and follow Jesus in crucifying our flesh, then we will be endued with the power of His resurrection. If we suffer with Him, we will be raised with Him, and then we can do the works that He did and even greater!

Not as though I had already attained, either were already perfect: but I follow after, if that I may apprehend that for which also I am apprehended of Christ Jesus.

Brethren, I count not myself to have apprehended: but this one thing I do, forgetting those things which are behind, and reaching forth unto those things which are before,

I press toward the mark for the prize of the high calling of God in Christ Jesus.

Philippians 3:12-14

I can tell you from personal experience, there is nothing better than pressing "toward the mark for the prize of the high calling of God in Christ Jesus." Like Paul, I wouldn't trade my life in Him for anything. Let me give you an example of one small but right choice I made that left me in awe of how much God cares about all of us.

I woke up in the night and knew I needed to call a pastor in Atlanta and ask him about a ministry he was sponsoring in Charlotte, but I went back to sleep. The next morning as I was eating breakfast, I remembered that I needed to call that pastor, so I obeyed the nudge from the Holy Spirit right then. "Bishop," he said, "I wanted to speak with you, but I'm going to meet with a couple this morning, and I didn't want to call you too early."

I said, "Well, that's funny. In the middle of the night, it came to me that I needed to talk to you." He couldn't believe that I'd called him. I couldn't believe he was ready to pick up the phone and call me about the very same issue. After we got through talking, I just smiled at myself. I thought, *I like this.* Don't you like those little surprises where God shows you He is with you, that He's working in your life and the lives of others?

God is calling the Church to maturity, to lay down our lives for Him and for each other. When we make the right choices to seek first His righteousness and not our youthful, selfish lusts, the Church will not only be mature, she will be powerful!

14

His Mighty Hand

Humble yourselves therefore under the mighty hand of God, that he may exalt you in due time:

Casting all your care upon him; for he careth for you.

1 Peter 5:6-7

Throughout the Bible, our Father is sometimes referred to as the potter, who molds us and makes us into the person He created us to be. When we resist Him and refuse to submit to His mighty hand, He leaves us to our own devices and lets the world humble us. This is always far more painful than submitting ourselves to His transforming power. He doesn't do this to be mean; He allows it because He respects our right to choose, even if we don't choose Him.

God loves us and wants us to be happy and successful in life, but He knows that will never happen if we don't grow up in Him. We decide whether we're going to be broken in pieces by wrong choices until we finally humble ourselves under God's mighty hand or if we're going to make the right choice to humble ourselves right away and stay humble. By the grace of God, I want to submit myself under the mighty hand of God every time.

It all started with Adam and Eve in the Garden of Eden. They made the wrong choice to obey Satan instead of God, and every human being since has been born with the sin nature. Satan became prince of the power of the air, god of this world, and ruler of spiritual darkness, wreaking havoc on human beings whenever he can. Even the physical realm was affected by sin. Everything began to die, colors faded, and nature became violent at times. Thank God that wasn't the last word!

God sent His only begotten Son Jesus to pay the price for sin with His sinless blood, and now we have a way to come back into divine order with God and His creation. Hallelujah! At the name of Jesus, every knee shall bow. The problem has been that the Church has lived like they are still subject to their flesh, the world, and the devil. We need to humble ourselves under the mighty hand of God instead of kowtowing to the enemy. We are the sons and daughters of the Most High God; the enemy is under our feet!

Until we get our resurrection bodies and are free of the old sin nature, we'll probably be a little rough around the edges, but that doesn't change who we are in Christ Jesus and what He has empowered us to do. He said that if we hunger and thirst after righteousness—making right choices—then we will be filled (Matthew 5:6). I want the Church to be filled!

I want us to be overflowing with God's integrity, compassion, and love. I want His power to be gushing out of us wherever we go. I want us to be so full of Him and His righteousness that we can't even conceive of making a wrong choice. That is what humbling ourselves under His mighty hand looks like.

I believe God is saying, "Okay, I've winked and looked the other way for a couple of thousand years, and now the time is really short. Playtime is over. We're in the last of the Last Days. Church, it's time to grow up and do the works of Jesus!"

Humility Toward Others

The minute someone talks about doing the works of Jesus, people always think of healing the sick, casting out demons, and raising the dead. Those are the works of Jesus. They're wonderful, and I want to be doing all those things. But all of these works mean nothing if the bride of Christ acts like a three year old.

Paul gives us a good example of what it looks like to humble ourselves and let God's love flow from us. He said, "If I eat meat and it offends my brother, I won't eat meat around him." He didn't say that he was sinning if he ate meat. He just said, "If my brother can't handle the fact that I eat meat because he thinks it's a sin or not healthy, I will humble myself and do the same. I don't want anything I do or not do to come between him and me or cause his faith in Jesus to falter."

> Therefore let us stop passing judgment on one another. Instead, make up your mind not to put any stumbling block or obstacle in the way of a brother or sister. I am convinced, being fully persuaded in the Lord Jesus, that nothing is unclean in itself. But if anyone regards something as unclean, then for that person it is unclean. If your brother or sister is distressed because of what you eat, you are no longer acting in love. Do not by your eating destroy someone for whom Christ died. Therefore do not let what you know is good be spoken of as evil. For the kingdom of God is not a matter of

eating and drinking, but of righteousness, peace and joy in the Holy Spirit, because anyone who serves Christ in this way is pleasing to God and receives human approval.

Romans 14:13-18 NIV

Some of us are not mature enough to do what Paul did. We are full of ourselves instead of the love of Christ and so we make fun of or look down on anyone who's different. "You don't eat meat? Well, that's your problem. I like meat and I'm going to eat it." Oh, aren't we mature!

Don't be fooled! Your actions and reactions in the natural speak of your maturity in the spiritual. I see folks do wild things, grown people who should know better. They are saints of God who have heard the Word and know what's right, but they say and do just the opposite. I can feel the Holy Spirit grieving. There's only so much you can do with a toddler, and there's only so much the Holy Spirit can do with a believer who refuses to grow up.

I know what you're thinking: The gifts of God are without repentance, which means immature believers do miracles. That's true, but eventually the Holy Spirit will pull them up and let them know that doing miracles does not mean they are okay and growing in the Lord. At that point, they have to decide if they're going to seek God's righteousness or become a dog-and-pony show. Eventually, if they don't grow up, they will probably fall.

If saints don't grow up, terrible things happen. They offend and run off the people who came to the Lord through them. Their family and personal life becomes a scandal and an embarrassment to the Church. If you think you can do your own thing and it won't affect anyone else, you are deceived. You are holding everyone back!

I'm speaking to myself as well as the Church when I say that we need to grow up and do the works of Jesus in all respects. I'm talking about the gifts of the Spirit working right alongside the fruit of the Spirit. We must become honorable miracle workers, honest healers, and disciplined deliverers. There's only one way that happens. We must make the right choice and humble ourselves under God's mighty hand.

Learning Obedience

Who in the days of his flesh, when he had offered up prayers and supplications with strong crying and tears unto him that was able to save him from death, and was heard in that he feared;

though he were a Son, yet learned he obedience by the things which he suffered;

and being made perfect, he became the author of eternal salvation unto all them that obey him.

Hebrews 5:7-9

This passage of scripture describes how Jesus learned obedience through suffering and the crucifixion of His flesh, yet believers think they should be exempt from all suffering and ought to be able to get away with "bending the rules" and "taking a little advantage." They forget that Jesus is their pattern. Jesus learned obedience, submission, respect, and duty in all the things He suffered. He is our responsible elder brother, and we can look to Him as a role model. It wasn't just the cross that caused Him to suffer. His own people made fun of Him. He was continually doubted and opposed. One of His closest friends betrayed Him and another denied Him. At one point, nearly everyone abandoned Him.

During the time He walked the earth, Jesus was vexed, hurt, and grieved, but He never whined, complained, or sinned in any way. Instead, He learned obedience. He humbled Himself under His Father's mighty hand and let His Father teach Him through His sufferings.

How could Jesus do that? He understood and lived by eternal truths, not temporary circumstances. What He knew He imparted to the apostle Paul, who wrote:

> For I reckon that the sufferings of this present time are not worthy to be compared with the glory which shall be revealed in us.
>
> **Romans 8:18**

> For our light affliction, which is but for a moment, worketh for us a far more exceeding and eternal weight of glory;
>
> While we look not at the things which are seen, but at the things which are not seen: for the things which are seen are temporal; but the things which are not seen are eternal.
>
> **2 Corinthians 4:17-18**

Paul understood what Jesus knew as He learned obedience through sufferings: glory awaits!

You say, "I seem to be learning obedience the hard way." Most of us do, but we don't have to. Jesus showed us a better way. We can be transformed by His Word and conduct our lives like He would. All we have to do is humble ourselves under God's mighty hand and seek His righteousness. Then we will learn obedience from any sufferings along the way and not only reap eternal rewards in glory but also enter into a glorious liberty in this life as well.

Glorious Liberty

The creature itself also shall be delivered from the bondage of corruption into the glorious liberty of the children of God.

Romans 8:21

If we seek God's righteousness and make right choices, we will come into a place of glorious liberty. I used to think glorious libery was signs and wonders and miracles; I want all that. But when I studied the word *liberty* in light of the Bible, I learned that liberty is the supernatural ability to omit things that have no relationship to salvation. Paul said this:

All things are lawful for me, but not all things are profitable. All things are lawful for me, but I will not be mastered by anything.

1 Corinthians 6:12 NASB

I'm not under law. I can eat anything, but not every food I want to eat is going to make me healthy. Some foods are going to make me sick. So even though all things are lawful for me, not all things are profitable. They aren't advantageous, practical, suitable, fit, or necessary.

Paul says that he will not be mastered by anything. If you are addicted to something, you are mastered by it. We shouldn't be mastered or ruled by anything or anyone but Jesus. He's your head—not a drug, alcohol, or a sexual attraction.

Can God trust you? Are you mature? Never mind what you'd like to think. Be honest! Have you resented your sufferings or have you learned obedience through them? How do you treat someone who irritates and frustrates you? Are you quick to pray and help those in need? Do you continuously build your faith through God's Word and prayer so that you are ready to believe Him for a miracle when it's needed? Are you quick to forgive and put away offenses? Do you quickly confess your sins to keep your slate clean with God?

If God blessed you with a lot of money, would you blow it on things you want or think you need, or would you ask God what to do with the money and then obey His instructions? If God can trust you with money, you are really trustworthy! Sometimes He gives us things just so we can see how mature we really are.

If God sent you a famous person who needed prayer, could He trust you to keep the person's problems and secrets to yourself, or would you call all the talk shows to tell them what you knew? None of us is perfect except Jesus, but if you are pressing into becoming a mature son or daughter of God, then He will be able to trust you with great responsibilities, especially when it comes to the people in your life. That's glorious liberty!

For, brethren, ye have been called unto liberty; only use not liberty for an occasion to the flesh, but by love serve one another.

For all the law is fulfilled in one word, even in this; Thou shalt love thy neighbour as thyself.

Galatians 5:13-14

Your liberty in Christ Jesus is not a freedom to sin; it means you are free of selfishness, free of lust, free of greed, free of the wicked tendencies and weaknesses that plagued you before you gave your life to God. If you are not seeking God's kingdom and His righteousness, then you are like a horse that is tied to a heavy cart. You are trying to go up the hill, but that heavy weight keeps dragging you back down. You need to make the right choice and cut off anything that is causing you to backslide, falter in your faith, or come under condemnation. That is not glorious liberty!

> **Then said Jesus to those Jews which believed on him, If ye continue in my word, then are ye my disciples indeed;**
>
> **And ye shall know the truth, and the truth shall make you free.**

John 8:31-32

The truth will make you free! It will make you free to be who He created you to be. Free to make right choices that are pleasing to Him and bring His power and blessing into your life. Lots of people quote verse 32, but they don't know that it hinges on verse 31: To be free, you must continue in the Word of God. You must grow up in Him to be truly free.

> **And the very God of peace sanctify you wholly; and I pray God your whole spirit and soul and body be preserved blameless unto the coming of our Lord Jesus Christ.**
>
> **Faithful is he that calleth you, who also will do it.**

1 Thessalonians 5:23-24

Paul is praying for God to sanctify us and says God is faithful to do it. He will cleanse you, separate you, and purify you through the washing of the water of His Word and the power of the Holy Spirit inside you. He will "sanctify you wholly." He won't just go half way, and He's not going to give up on you. He wants you whole and free and walking in His glorious liberty.

Paul goes on to pray that "your whole spirit and soul and body be preserved blameless unto the coming of our Lord Jesus

Christ." God wants to preserve you, but not in all your faults, weaknesses, and sins. He wants to clear those out of your spirit, soul, and body so that you are preserved blameless. He doesn't want you to stand before Him with any wrong choices in your account.

When we stand before Jesus Christ, we may have gone through fires, floods, and relationship problems. If we have been making right choices, humbling ourselves under the mighty hand of God, we will be ready to see Him because we will have become like Him. That's glorious liberty!

15

Unbelievable Courage

What is on the inside of you is going to become evident; that is your fruit. If you have been making right choices, living like the righteous child of God you are, the fruit of your life will evidence that fact. What such fruit look like?

I have been young, and now am old; yet have I not seen the righteous forsaken, nor his seed begging bread.

Psalm 37:25

If you find yourself pleading with God or on the street begging, you might take a good look at the choices that got you there. I believe when you love the Lord and serve Him, you will be blessed, and your right choices will bring God's blessing on the generations that come after you as well. This is especially true if you raised your children and grandchildren in the Lord.

I found out a few years ago that my great-grandmother was Spirit filled. My aunt said that her mother (my grandmother) told her that when she was a little child during the Civil War, many times she would wake up in the night and hear her mother (my great-grandmother) praying in other tongues for her family to be safe and protected. They lived in a log cabin, grew a garden to eat, and had a gun to keep the Indians away while the men were out fighting. I think my great-grandmother is dancing for joy in Heaven that the prayers she sowed for her generations to come brought me along to preach the gospel. Now, I pray for my seed. If Jesus tarries, I want my family to be blessed with the fruit of my right choices.

> **As righteousness tendeth to life: so he that pursueth evil pursueth it to his own death.**
>
> **Though hand join in hand, the wicked shall not be unpunished: but the seed of the righteous shall be delivered.**
>
> **Proverbs 11:19, 21**

God promises that our offspring shall be delivered. They may not be able to avoid trouble, but they will see the delivering hand of the Lord working in their lives.

Such wonderful fruit comes from our right choices.

- Clear conscience
- Inner peace and contentment
- Satisfaction and success
- Joy from pleasing the Lord
- Abundant life
- Overcoming sins, faults, and weaknesses
- Enemies make peace with you
- Knowing the Lord more intimately
- Being a good witness for Jesus to others

- Doing the works of Jesus
- Becoming more like Jesus, a mature son or daughter
- Enjoying glorious liberty in Him

> **See then that ye walk circumspectly, not as fools, but as wise.**
>
> **Ephesians 5:15**

As we see this fruit coming forth in our lives, we must live circumspectly, accurately, diligently, thoughtfully, carefully; not as fools and the unwise. Here's what the Bible says about fools:

> **The fool hath said in his heart, There is no God. They are corrupt, they have done abominable works, there is none that doeth good.**
>
> **Psalm 14:1**

Fools say, "I'll never have to answer for what I say or do because there is no God." They believe they are their own god and will never reap the consequences of their wrong choices. In fact, many don't care whether or not they make right choices. Those who are wise know what the will of the Lord is and they do it.

> **Wherefore be ye not unwise, but understanding what the will of the Lord is.**
>
> **Ephesians 5:17**

> **And be not drunk with wine, wherein is excess; but be filled with the Spirit.**
>
> **Ephesians 5:18**

We must be filled, overflowing, and complete with the Holy Spirit. Be bursting out with the Spirit! Don't put yourself under the influence of anything that messes with your mind or drives you to do something wrong that you wouldn't normally do.

I beseech you therefore, brethren, by the mercies of God, that ye present your bodies a living sacrifice, holy, acceptable unto God, which is your reasonable service.

And be not conformed to this world: but be ye transformed by the renewing of your mind, that ye may prove what is that good, and acceptable, and perfect, will of God.

Romans 12:1-2

We are not to use drugs or alcohol to be transformed into someone we are not! We are to be transformed by the renewing of our mind with God's Word. According to Strong's Concordance, that word *transformed* is translated from the Greek word *metamorphoo*, which is where we get the word *metamorphosis*. It means you go through a process of becoming the person God created you to be.

A worm is not destined to stay a worm. That worm goes through a process of cooperating with God's design for its life and builds a cocoon around itself so that God can do a miracle as it bursts out of that cocoon as a beautiful butterfly, flying free.

Believers build a cocoon of God's Word and the power of the Holy Spirit around themselves so that He can do a miracle, making them into the image of Christ Jesus and giving them the ability to do the works of Jesus. Now that is awesome fruit!

Sometimes what we consider good fruit is not what God considers to be good fruit, so we must always seek His kingdom and His righteousness, not our own. In Genesis, chapter 4, Cain thought his grain offering was acceptable, but it wasn't. God had no respect for Cain's offering, but He respected Abel's sacrifice of a lamb. Abel made the right choice.

Cain got mad and was jealous of his brother, but God gave Cain another chance. He said, "If you make the right choice, all will be well. But if you make the wrong choice, sin lies at the door." As you know, Cain made another unrighteous choice. He refused to humble himself, and sin was right there waiting for him. Satanic pride became his guide, and he killed his brother Abel.

Don't go the way of Cain! Swallow your pride, crucify your flesh, and make the right choice. That's the mark of a mature son or daughter of God.

Dunamis

Paul spoke of the power of the believer in Ephesians, chapter 1. He prayed for all of us to know "what is the exceeding greatness of his power to us-ward who believe" (v. 19). The Greek word *dunamis* is translated *power*, and it is exceeding—growing and multiplying —giving believers a constant supply of supernatural strength, ability, moral power, and excellence of soul, according to Strong's Concordance. It imparts power of influence, power of resources, and miracle-working power. That's a whole lot of power! Dunamis gives us the divine ability to make right choices and carry them out, whether it's resisting temptation or raising the dead. Dunamis is the grace of God activated in a believer's life. We can do all things through Christ, who strengths us (Philippians 4:13)!

Have you ever gone through something you didn't think you could endure? I have, many times! In the midst of a terrible trial, as I was crying out to God and clinging to Him to just take one more breath or one more step, I was able to go beyond what I thought I was capable of doing. How did I make it? It was nothing I or anybody else did. There was something supernatural that brought me through that trial. It was dunamis! God's miracle power was working exceedingly in me.

Where does this power reside in you? This power is found in the person of the Holy Spirit, who lives in your spirit. When you received Jesus as your Lord and Savior, you received His Holy Spirit, His divine ability and power. Now you can function in your daily life because you have the exceeding greatness of His power in you. This is a mind-blowing revelation when you really get it!

When I received God's power, I received His strength, His ability, His moral excellence, His power of influence, His power of resources, and His miracle-working power. So when I read what Jesus commanded all of us to do, just before He ascended to His Father's right hand in Heaven, I know I can draw upon this power to give me a courage that is unbelievable.

> **And he said unto them, Go ye into all the world, and preach the gospel to every creature.**
>
> **He that believeth and is baptized shall be saved; but he that believeth not shall be damned.**
>
> **And these signs shall follow them that believe; In my name shall they cast out devils; they shall speak with new tongues;**
>
> **they shall take up serpents; and if they drink any deadly thing, it shall not hurt them; they shall lay hands on the sick, and they shall recover.**
>
> **Mark 16:15-18**

Imagine standing right in front of Jesus as He is commanding you to do all these things. He's telling you to go head-to-head with the devil and all his demons, confront the world and all its deceptions and persecution, and crucify the minefield of your flesh that wants to do nothing but sin. Ministering the gospel is a dangerous business!

Matthew recorded the scene this way:

> **And when they saw him, they worshipped him: but some doubted.**
>
> **And Jesus came and spake unto them, saying, All power is given unto me in heaven and in earth.**
>
> **Go ye therefore, and teach all nations, baptizing them in the name of the Father, and of the Son, and of the Holy Ghost:**
>
> **Teaching them to observe all things whatsoever I have commanded you: and, lo, I am with you always, even unto the end of the world. Amen.**
>
> Matthew 28:17-20

Did you notice? Some doubted. They were like us. They wondered how they could possibly do the works of Jesus. But Jesus told them He had all power and authority over the enemy, the world, and their flesh. They could do what He was commanding in His strength. Just when they were starting to get some courage, He said, "Oh, and by the way, I want you to teach all nations. Baptize them (which means get them saved) and teach them to live according to My Word." This was another tall order!

Those gathered to hear these words probably thought, "How is all this going to happen if You're leaving?" Well, Luke's gospel tells us something else Jesus said to the group before He ascended to the Father:

And, behold, I send the promise of my Father upon you: but tarry ye in the city of Jerusalem, until ye be endued with power from on high.

Luke 24:49

Jesus said, "Don't go anywhere or do anything until you are endued with power from on high." That word for *power* is *dunamis!* The way they could do everything Jesus commanded—the way you can do it, too—is through the exceeding greatness of His power that dwells within believers. You have the same power that raised Jesus from the dead living in you.

My Testimony

When I came to the Lord, I was a little child. As I was growing up, there were times when I didn't really feel saved. Every time the preacher gave an altar call, I wanted to go get saved again, just to make sure. On top of that, nobody was more timid than I. My sister would tell my parents that I embarrassed her. When she'd have her friends over to the house, I'd stutter when I said, "Hello," and hold my hand over my face. I couldn't look at her friends. I was so scared.

What happened to me? How did that shy, little girl become a preaching dynamo? The dunamis power of the Holy Spirit came into me! At sixteen, I attended a tent meeting on a Saturday afternoon. The next morning, I discovered I could speak and act with a confidence I had never had before. That Sunday morning, I got up and was getting ready to go to church. I had never seen my father in church. He'd never talked about God or questioned where I was going, but that morning he asked, "Where are you going to church?"

I answered, "Well, we're going over to Brother Roloff's church." My father was livid. "You will not go to that church! It's a Baptist church! You won't leave this house till you promise me you're not going to that church!"

Everybody in town knew Brother Roloff. People would say, "He preached every Pentecostal church full." That's the kind of preacher he was. But now, I had to promise my father I wouldn't go to his church. Now remember, I got the Holy Spirit the day before. I didn't know what kind of power I'd received.

Tearfully, I met my boyfriend and said, "We can't go over there to church."

He said, "Where are we going?"

I said, "Well, that tent I was at yesterday had some preachers on the platform, and one of them said he pastored the Corpus Christi Tabernacle. Let's go over there." I went from the frying pan into the fire! That preacher taught on receiving the grace of God. You need the grace of God in your life. At the end of the service, he had everybody bow their heads. He said, "If you need the grace of God in your life, hold up your hand." Well, my daddy had just taken me to task and had me in tears, so I held up my hand ever so slightly, so no one would notice me.

Then the preacher said, "If you really need the grace of God, stand up." Well, there's no way you can hide if you stand up. But I needed God so badly that morning, an unbelievable courage rose up in me and I stood up. I knew I was incapable of doing that on my own. Later, I was able to break off my engagement with the young man I'd attended the service with that morning because he didn't want to serve the Lord. That boy was everything to me—until I received unbelievable courage to make right choices. God knew I was going to need it!

I became the youth president at the church, and we had a little fifteen-minute radio program on Saturdays. I was the speaker! I knew that my daddy would find out sooner or later what I was doing, so I decided to tell him. It was the right thing to do. I told him after he had eaten supper, and he was furious. He said, "You're going to make me lose my job. Are you able to support me in the manner to which I'm accustomed? Leave this house!" I picked up my purse and my keys by the door and walked out. He stood there and called out after me, "You don't need to ever come back to this house." I knew he meant it.

How did I stand up to him like that? Where did I get the courage and the strength to leave? The power of the Holy Spirit in me was greater than anything I was facing in the world (1 John 4:4). In Him I could do what I never could do in my natural ability and strength, and you can too! You can smile through persecution for the gospel's sake. You can love people who aren't kind or good to you. You can keep yourself pure in a wicked world.

After breaking off my engagement, not only was I able to wait a number of years for God's choice of a husband, but I had the courage to marry him even when my family was against it. They heard that John had been a drug addict before he got saved. Then they heard his last name was Gimenez. That was it for them! The night before I was married, my mother called and told me, "If you've just got to have a man, why don't you marry a white man?"

I said, "God has kept me thirty-five years. I don't "just have to have a man." God has kept me for *this* man."

Then my father got on the phone and said terrible things, causing tears to run down my face. John kept saying, "Hang up. You don't have to listen to that."

I said, "No. They've got a right. They think they're trying to save my life. They've got a right to say anything they want to say to me, and then I have to choose."

My mother said, "If you walk down that aisle and stand before a preacher, I curse your marriage. I curse it. And I'll never call you by your married name." Well, I walked down that aisle and married John. If she did curse us, we never felt it. We knew we were in God's will.

Looking back, I marvel at what I did in faith. Before I was married, I drove all over the country by myself. (I did carry a little 22 caliber automatic pistol in a cosmetic purse on the seat right beside me. I'm from Texas, and back then, they didn't say anything about a permit!) I stayed in other people's houses all over the country. They could have been axe murderers and killed me. How did I have the courage to do that? The power of the Holy Spirit gave me unbelievable courage.

I remember a night in Canada. A man had invited me to come up there and preach in his church that was meeting in the YMCA. He said, "God told me there's going to be miracles tonight."

I thought, *Oh really?*

He continued, "And you're going to pray for the miracles."

At first I thought, *Pray for your own miracles. Leave me out of it.* But then I thought, *If he's got enough gall to tell me to get up there and pray, I'm going to act and pray like I know what I'm doing.*

I gave the call for prayer and the people came three and four deep all across the front. I just started praying for them, believing for them to be touched by God. Lo and behold, I became a great miracle worker that night!

A couple of years ago, a man came to our church and said, "Do you remember one night in Toronto, Canada, at the YMCA, when you prayed for miracles?"

I thought, *Boy do I remember!* He said, "I'm one of those miracles."

This shy little girl who couldn't even say hello to a stranger, now had the courage to stand up for the truth with her parents, travel across the country by herself, stay with strangers in their homes, boldly preach the Gospel, and pray for miracles she then saw happen. How could this be? I can tell you, it was not me! It was the dunamis power of the Holy Spirit. Spirit

Your Commission

Daniel 11:32 says that those who know God, who have experienced His love and power, and who make right choices that please Him, will be strong and do great exploits. They will have unbelievable courage.

- It takes unbelievable courage to tell unbelievers that they will go to hell if they don't receive Jesus as their Lord and Savior.

- It takes unbelievable courage to stop at a car accident and pray for the injured to be healed.

- It takes unbelievable courage to walk up to a homeless beggar who is yelling and screaming like a mad person and cast the demons out of him.

- It takes unbelievable courage to ask forgiveness for something you are ashamed of, something you don't want anyone to know you said or did.

- It takes unbelievable courage to live like Jesus instead of thinking, talking, and behaving like the people of your world, to bring God's culture to the society in which you live.

- It takes unbelievable courage to speak the truth in love to a brother or sister who is in sin or has embraced heresy.

God has given you unbelievable courage to do all these things and more. All you have to do is make right choices!

16

The Price Is Right

But ye shall receive power, after that the Holy Ghost is come upon you: and ye shall be witnesses unto me both in Jerusalem, and in all Judaea, and in Samaria, and unto the uttermost part of the earth.

Acts 1:8

What is this unbelievable courage meant for? Why does God fill you and endue you with power from on high? It is so you can be Jesus' witness. A witness for Jesus lives in such a way as to authenticate Him, declare Him, testify of Him, validate Him, prove Him, confirm Him, and attest to Him. Jesus gave you His Holy Spirit so you could be His witness in your family, your schools, your neighborhood, your city, your nation, and throughout the earth.

Look at Peter, the coward who denied Jesus three times. He got up and preached the gospel to thousands on the Day of Pentecost. Some of those people had just crucified Jesus—and he reminded them that they had! Peter went from being a coward to being a mighty witness for the Lord Jesus Christ. You have received that same power to be Jesus' witness.

Take a moment to consider all the things you have done for Jesus that you know could not have been done without the power of the Holy Spirit. Even if you just got saved, you know you couldn't have made that choice to go from the kingdom of darkness and all your old friends and beliefs to the kingdom of God—where Jesus is Lord and you're not! You needed His grace and faith and the power of the Holy Spirit to make that first righteous decision.

If you have faithfully followed the Lord for any length of time, you probably have had times when you thought, *I can't do this. I don't think I can make it through this.* When those times came, you simply made the right choice to put your life and the lives of your loved ones in God's hands as you trusted Him in faith. As you made that choice, He rose up in you. The next thing you knew, you were doing and experiencing what you thought was impossible.

The Bible is full of stories of ordinary people who did extraordinary things, and church historians have written of all the faithful saints through the centuries who worked miracles and stood strong for Jesus in the face of horrific persecution, torture, and death. The world called them righteous because they made right choices. I guarantee you, every one of them did their best to love and serve the Lord in every situation. I can also guarantee you that those who succeeded, suffered for it.

In our era, some thought they could never admit their sin and be forgiven, yet they found the courage to do that and were set free. Some thought they would die under torture and persecution, but they lived to give their testimony. Others lost friends, were ostracized from their families, but found a new life in Jesus. Some began their walk with the Lord expecting their lives to go a certain way, only to find He was taking them in a totally different direction. And yet, they still went on loving and serving Him.

Was the price these people paid right? Do you think it was fair?

What about you? Do you think you've paid too high a price to follow the Lord, or do you think He has been fair with you? Are you willing to go into the future making the right choices to please God with your life, no matter what it costs you?

As you're considering your answer, picture the cross. There He is, the Son of God, bleeding, gasping for breath, and pouring out His life for you. He was beaten, spit upon, mocked, and ridiculed. Everyone but His mother, a couple of women, and the apostle John abandoned Him. The men He spent hours studying the Holy Scriptures with from the time He was a boy were the very ones who had Him arrested and beaten. He was rejected, betrayed, tortured. He took every sin upon Himself so that you could become righteous, whole, and at peace with the Creator of the Universe.

When I consider all these things, I can't help but believe the price of righteousness is right! In whatever way I can, I will pour out my life for the Lord and King who poured out His life for me.

Reasonable Service

I beseech you therefore, brethren, by the mercies of God, that ye present your bodies a living sacrifice, holy, acceptable unto God, which is your reasonable service.

Romans 12:1

The apostle Paul wrote these words under the unction of the Holy Spirit. He begs us to live a godly life and declares that this is not an unreasonable request. Laying down your life for Jesus is reasonable. It's logical. It makes sense. There is nothing outrageous or extreme about it. It is exactly what you should do, because Jesus poured out His life for you. Every blessing and success you have is because you received His great salvation through His sacrifice. It isn't because you are such a smart, good-looking, wonderful person! Every goodness in you and every blessing you have is because of Him.

And be not conformed to this world: but be ye transformed by the renewing of your mind, that ye may prove what is that good, and acceptable, and perfect, will of God.

Romans 12:2

The popular and exciting game show called *The Price Is Right*, has been on television since the 1950s. Contestants are put in various situations where they have to guess the price of something. The one who gets the closest wins that round or the big prize.

In Romans 12:2, Paul speaks about the good, acceptable, and perfect will of God. How much do you think it will cost you to live in that will? What value do you place on living a life that is "good," "acceptable," and "perfect"? Do you just want to get saved from hell, do you want to get saved and just do what's necessary, or do you want to go all the way and do God's perfect will?

Making right choices is always the good, acceptable, and perfect will of God.

We should make right choices because we love God. When He asks us to do something, we do it because His will is always good, acceptable, and perfect. His way is best.

When Paul stood before King Agrippa and was permitted to speak, he wasn't afraid or ashamed. He was carrying out his righteous decision to do the good, acceptable, and perfect will of God.

Paul was subject to the same passions, fears, and insecurities as we are, but in Acts 26:2, he said, "I think myself happy, king Agrippa, because I shall answer for myself this day before thee touching all the things whereof I am accused of the Jews." Paul boldly gave his testimony and told the Agrippa the Good News of Jesus Christ. He explained that he was able to do all this, "Having therefore obtained help of God" (Acts 26:22). Today he would have said, "Wasn't me! It was all God!"

Paul thought it completely reasonable, logical, and sensible to make right choices that manifested the good, acceptable, and perfect will of God. As an apostle, he considered it an honor, a privilege, and a joy to stand strong for Jesus through anything. Paul gives us a list of what some of that "anything" encompassed in his life:

Of the Jews five times received I forty stripes save one.

Thrice was I beaten with rods, once was I stoned, thrice I suffered shipwreck, a night and a day I have been in the deep;

In journeyings often, in perils of waters, in perils of robbers, in perils by mine own countrymen, in perils by the heathen, in perils in the city, in perils in the wilderness, in perils in the sea, in perils among false brethren;

In weariness and painfulness, in watchings often, in hunger and thirst, in fastings often, in cold and nakedness.

2 Corinthians 11:24-27

These are what Paul called "light afflictions" (2 Corinthians 4:17)! If you live in America, you probably have not experienced most of the things on this list (though in the future you might). If you live in other countries, you may have experienced these things. But we all have the divine ability to be a witness just like Paul.

What Manner of Love

Behold, what manner of love the Father hath bestowed upon us, that we should be called the sons of God.

1 John 3:1

When people say, "I'm mad at God," my mouth drops open. I want to say, "You little peanut. You're mad at God? You didn't get your way, and now you're whining? What you need is some power to submit, to lay low before God and say, 'Not my will but Thine be done!'"

I was preaching in a church in New York City called Rock Church. They had a little apartment for the evangelist upstairs from the church, and I was praying before I was to preach. I said, "God, I want to see the miracles Jesus saw."

God answered me: "Live the life He lived."

Jesus lived a "Not my will but Thine be done," kind of life. He was one hundred percent God's right-choice man. Some of the things Christians complain about are not reasonable, logical, or at all sensible in light of what God has done for us. If you're one of those Christians, it's time for you to wake up!

Jesus is often portrayed as a mild-mannered lover of people who would never consider allowing one of His beloved to go to a fiery furnace or a den of lions. Oops, He already did that! You may say, "Well that was the Old Testament. In the New Testament He saves us from all that."

But does He?

After these things the Lord appointed other seventy also, and sent them two and two before his face into every city and place, whither he himself would come.

Go your ways: behold, I send you forth as lambs among wolves.

Carry neither purse, nor scrip, nor shoes: and salute no man by the way.

And into whatsoever house ye enter, first say, Peace be to this house.

Luke 10:1, 3-5

Jesus sent His lambs among wolves without money or shoes! He forced them to rely completely upon God for everything they needed to survive and to do His works.

Remember the word that I said unto you, The servant is not greater than his lord. If they have persecuted me, they will also persecute you.

John 15:20

These things I have spoken unto you, that in me ye might have peace. In the world ye shall have tribulation: but be of good cheer; I have overcome the world.

John 16:33

Jesus told us the truth. He said we will be persecuted and have tribulation, but no matter what we experience, we will always have His peace inside us. We can be assured that whatever we face, He has supplied all our needs and has overcome it. What manner of love is this? It is the greatest love—unconditional, *agape* love that comes only from God!

I was in a meeting in Atlanta, Georgia, with maybe five thousand people who were gathered for a healing service. A man whose left arm was in a sling went up for prayer. I could see his hand coming out of the sling, and it was as black as pitch. He told the evangelist, "I fell through a plate glass door. The glass nearly cut my arm off; the only thing that was holding it on was just a little piece of skin and the bone. I had the doctor sew my arm back on, but they are telling me that if I don't let them amputate within the next twenty-four hours, I will die of blood poisoning. They will not be able to stop the progress of gangrene in my arm."

The evangelist asked the man, "Who brought you here?"

The man said, "My wife. She's a Christian."

The evangelist asked, "Are you a believer?"

The man said, "No."

The evangelist looked at him and said, "If God heals you, will you serve Him?"

The man said, "Yes, I will."

The evangelist prayed for the man. I saw real color come into his hand until it looked normal. The next night, the man was back in the meeting with the sling off, and he was praising the Lord.

If Jesus heals you, will you serve Him?

More to the point, since He saved you from eternal damnation and hell, from a life of futility, confusion, rejection, rage, and fear of just about everything—will you serve Him?

What manner of love has He shown you? Now, what manner of love do you show Him?

What We'll See

Jesus pointed us to the time when our trials and tribulations in a fallen world—with a devil and his demons running rampant and our old sin nature trying to trip us up at every turn—would cease.

And ye now therefore have sorrow: but I will see you again, and your heart shall rejoice, and your joy no man taketh from you.

John 16:22

The next time we see our Savior face-to-face on this earth, we will be in our resurrection bodies, the devil will be gone, and everything and everyone will be under the rule of the Lord Jesus Christ. Don't ask me how it's all going to work. Frankly, I don't care! He's coming back, and I know He will set everything right because He is the King of righteousness and the Lord of right choices!

The only thing I care about is that when He sees me, when He beholds His bride the Church, He will see what Solomon saw.

Who is this that cometh up from the wilderness, leaning upon her beloved?

My dove, my undefiled is but one; she is the only one of her mother, she is the choice one of her that bare her. The daughters saw her, and blessed her; yea, the queens and the concubines, and they praised her.

Who is she that looketh forth as the morning, fair as the moon, clear as the sun, and terrible as an army with banners?

Song of Solomon 8:5; 6:9-10

Are we leaning completely on Him?

Are we undefiled, blessed, and praised?

Are we seeing what He sees?

Are we fair, clear, and a mighty army to be reckoned with?

If we are making right choices by seeking first His kingdom and His righteousness, then this is what Jesus will see! Hallelujah!

Father, I pray for the readers of this book and ask You to stir their hearts to repent of any sin, to recommit their lives to You, and to set their hearts to seek first Your kingdom and Your righteousness in all they think, say, and do. Thank You for giving them Your Holy Spirit who imparts unbelievable courage, so that they can stand strong and be a powerful witness for the Gospel of Jesus Christ in their world. Kindle a fire in them to live every day making right choices for You.

In Jesus' mighty name, I pray Your love, blessings, honor, and glory upon their lives. Amen.

PRAYER OF SALVATION

God loves you—no matter who you are, no matter what your past. God loves you so much that He gave His one and only begotten Son for you. The Bible tells us that "...whoever believes in him shall not perish but have eternal life" (John 3:16 NIV). Jesus laid down His life and rose again so that we could spend eternity with Him and experience His absolute best on earth. If you would like to receive Jesus into your life, say the following prayer out loud and mean it in your heart.

Heavenly Father, I come to you admitting that I am a sinner. Right now, I choose to turn away from sin, and I ask you to cleanse me of all unrighteousness. I believe that Your son, Jesus, died on the cross to take away my sins. I also believe that He rose again from the dead so that I might be forgiven of my sins and made righteous through faith in Him. I call upon the name of Jesus Christ to be the Savior and Lord of my life. Jesus, I choose to follow You and ask that You fill me with the power of the Holy Spirit. I declare that right now I am a child of God. I am free from sin and full of the righteousness of God. I am saved in Jesus' name. Amen.

If you prayed this prayer to receive Jesus Christ as your Savior for the first time, please write to us to receive a free book!

www.harrisonhouse.com
Harrison House Publishers
P.O. Box 35035
Tulsa, Oklahoma 74153

The Harrison House Vision

Proclaiming the truth and the power

Of the Gospel of Jesus Christ

With excellence;

Challenging Christians to

Live victoriously,

Grow spiritually,

Know God intimately.